THE MODERN NATIONS IN

HISTORICAL PERSPECTIVE

ROBIN W. WINKS, *General Editor*

The volumes in this series deal with individual nations or groups of closely related nations throughout the world, summarizing the chief historical trends and influences that have contributed to each nation's present-day character, problems, and behavior. Recent data are incorporated with established historical background to achieve a fresh synthesis and original interpretation.

The author of this volume, WILLIAM J. CAMERON, is a *Pakeha* New Zealander. A scholar who takes great interest in the interrelationship of history and literature, Dr. Cameron is Professor of English at McMaster University in Ontario. He is the author of *New Light on Aphra Behn* and editor of the forthcoming *Poems on Affairs of State,* Volume V.

FORTHCOMING COMMONWEALTH VOLUMES
Australia *by Russel Ward* (Published 1965)
British East Africa *by Colin T. Leys*
Canada *by Frank Underhill*
Central Africa *by Prosser Gifford*
Ceylon *by S. Arasaratnam* (Published 1964)
Ghana and Nigeria *by John Flint*
Great Britain *by Norman Cantor*
India *by Stanley Wolpert*
Malaysia *by John Bastin*
Sierre Leone and Liberia *by Christopher Fyfe*
The West Indian Islands *by D. A. G. Waddell*

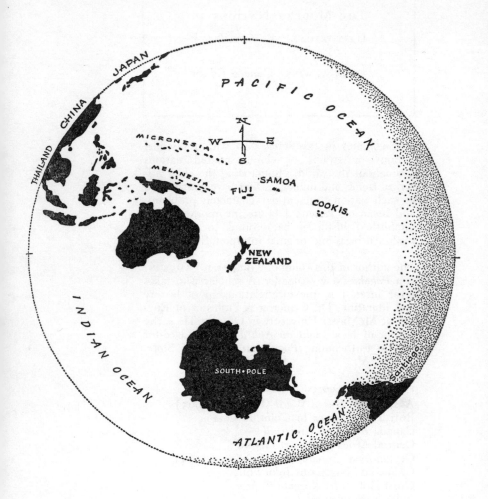

NEW ZEALAND

WILLIAM J. CAMERON

A SPECTRUM BOOK

Prentice-Hall, Inc.

Englewood Cliffs, New Jersey

Current printing (last digit):

12 11 10 9 8 7 6 5 4 3

No single national history, in relation to size, population, and duration, has been so thoroughly or so well written as New Zealand's progressive story. New Zealanders are among the most literate people in the world, and they consume books about themselves more rapidly than do the citizens of any other country. Certainly, the number of books on New Zealand—general interpretations, local histories, and specialists' monographs—far outnumber, proportionately, those on any other member of the Commonwealth of Nations. Why, then, another history of New Zealand?

Dr. Cameron has recognized an important historical truth: if one is to understand a country, one must know what its people argue about, why they argue, and how. He also knows that a nation is not to be measured by its present powers or by its territorial ambitions but, rather, by its goals. Accordingly, Dr. Cameron has written a series of interrelated essays in which he speaks, queries, and answers as a New Zealander does. He is not an historian but a student of literature, and he has chosen to pose his questions in a literary way, from the sources. In doing so, he has written a uniquely personal essay on what he finds right and also wrong in this most British of Dominions.

Dr. Cameron examines New Zealand attitudes toward the indigenous Maori. He explores the effect of the welfare state on national character. Because new ideas first come into conflict with the traditional in schools, he writes at length of New Zealand's educational system. Because industrial progress often precedes changes in prevailing ideas, he examines the nature of New Zealand's industry and explores carefully two case studies in New Zealand success and failure: timber and glass. Because geography often determines or limits human action, he relates New Zealand's highly

v

diverse regional nature to its equally diverse human characteristics. Because New Zealanders are an uncommonly literate lot, he emphasizes the books which have most influenced New Zealand national thought. In order to permit a more thorough exploration of these themes, much is omitted here that traditionally would be present.

His exploration of the history of his native country is thus highly original—at once interpretive and explanatory, of great interest to the New Zealander and of great use to the reader who wishes to begin learning of New Zealand here. What students of the Pacific, of Britain, of New Zealand, and of the Empire-Commonwealth have long needed is a personal interpretation of New Zealand's national character, by a New Zealand scholar, and this Dr. Cameron has set out to supply.

Robin W. Winks
Series Editor

While spending a rewarding year in the United States as a visiting scholar, I found myself continually being called upon to explain to interested American friends what New Zealand and her people are like, what part New Zealand plays in world affairs, what hopes New Zealanders had for her future, and so on. This book is an attempt to set down in a more systematic and better-informed way an elaboration of my tentative answers to such persistent questioning. It is in fact a personal essay, with many of the defects, but (one hopes) some of the advantages of the genre.

Anyone who wants to have the facts about New Zealand may dip into the current edition of the *New Zealand Official Yearbook*, or, if the 1200 or so pages are too indigestible, may consult the excellent text and maps in A *Descriptive Atlas of New Zealand* (ed. A. H. McLintock), 1959. But both these essential sources of information have an aura of objective authority that seems to act as a barrier to understanding. Throughout this essay, therefore, I have attempted to keep in mind an image of an intelligent American friend probing, probing, probing, trying to clarify for himself through personal mediation the meaning of what is conveyed in such severely official volumes. As the questioner probes for the reasonable and reasoned basis of the opinions he hears, I take it that his informant should refer him to the most helpful books on the topic (with brief personal judgments on their value) and, where no reliable study exists, must try his best to supply the deficiency. This "best" cannot be really satisfactory without years of special research, but an amateurish effort may help to indicate where such research is most needed. Because of the largely undeveloped state of certain fields of scholarly study (such as sociology) and the lopsided emphasis in others (such as in the vital field of history), even the most perceptive and sensitive of New Zealand's intelligentsia would find it difficult to produce a reasonably-balanced synoptic view of the actuality and potentiality of his small and young nation. However, a greater quantity of scholarly work on New Zealand has appeared in the past two decades than ever before, and the next decade may be even more fruitful. As the world is changing fast, we cannot wait for this harvest, and any honest attempt to take stock of our present position in terms of the past should be welcome. This extended personal essay is therefore offered in the hope that it will help readers to gauge how much and how successfully New Zealand may be called upon to take part in the affairs of the world in the near future.

W. J. C.

CONTENTS

ix

ONE

NEW ZEALAND, THE COMMONWEALTH,

AND THE WORLD

Ties Through War and Sport

In almost every New Zealand town there is a monument to the strongest, most instinctive, and possibly most important tie that binds New Zealanders to the outside world. At a commanding point stands the war memorial: sometimes a stern monolith, sometimes a plaque set into the wall of a community hall or into a gateway leading to a memorial park, recreation field, or "garden of remembrance." In the more opulent or more populous towns, the monument is frequently a warlike, pensive, or courageous figure in the uniform of the World War of 1914-18, with a characteristic "lemon-squeezer" hat. The monument may even be a building (in Auckland it is the War Memorial Museum), but whatever form it takes, on it will be inscribed the names of those who died in Gallipoli, Flanders, Syria, Egypt, and diverse places on the far side of the world. The lists are surprisingly long for such a sparsely-populated country, indicating a remarkably deep involvement in that distant war. Added to the old roster, or inscribed nearby, will be a somewhat shorter list of other men and women who died between 1939 and 1945; this list is likely to include numerous European and Middle Eastern place names, but sprinkled among them one will note many an Asian or Pacific locality.

In 1939, the Prime Minister summed up the instinctive sentiments of the people of the Dominion of New Zealand when he seconded

1

Britain's declaration of war against Germany with the words, "Behind the sure shield of Britain we have enjoyed and cherished freedom and self-government. . . . Where she goes, we go. Where she stands, we stand." Without hesitation, most New Zealanders took for granted the assumption that this sentiment would be translated into action by sending a large force to Europe or the Middle East. The country recalled the experience of the First World War, when 16,000 of the 100,000 who served overseas died—the highest death rate of any British Commonwealth country—and another 41,000 were wounded or injured in a tangible demonstration of loyalty to Britain, though the population of New Zealand had not yet reached 1,200,000. The community was deeply aware of its commitments in Europe and the Middle East, and the ties thus forged would not—and will not now—be broken easily.

Even in the Second World War, areas geographically nearer home did not take on the emotional significance of the battlefields on the other side of the globe. Indeed, when Australia (against Britain's wishes) withdrew her troops from the Middle East after the war spread to the Pacific, the New Zealand Second Division remained in North Africa, and a Third Division was rapidly organized for service in the Pacific. The pride that some New Zealanders felt and expressed in connection with this act of altruism was ill-based (after all, both Australia and the United States of America provided amply for New Zealand's defense), but it does illustrate how strong the feelings of loyalty to Britain were. National pride was hurt, too, by the Allied decision in 1943-44 to withdraw the Third Division from the Pacific, but the war effort was quickly concentrated upon maintaining one division in Europe and producing food and raw materials for Britain and for the enormous fighting force deployed in the South Pacific.

The "invasion" of New Zealand by friendly American troops and the smooth transfer of British and New Zealand warships to American command were obvious signs of a revolution in the making. For the first time in the twentieth century, New Zealand became deeply aware of her unique regional and strategical interests. Yet, for a number of years the needs of Britain, the needs of the United States, and her own needs were in almost perfect harmony. To safeguard her independent interests even before this new situation developed, however,

New Zealand had made a step toward establishing her own diplomatic service. A minister was sent to Washington in 1941. (Later, in 1944, a short-lived Legation was also established in Moscow.) Symptomatically, the Imperial Affairs Section of the Prime Minister's Department was in 1943 reorganized and expanded to form the Department of External Affairs. Nineteen years later, members of this Department presented papers on their work to the annual Convention of the Institute of Public Administration, and the results were published in book form.[1]

Undoubtedly, New Zealanders value their record overseas in the field of sport almost as much as their record in war. Rugby football is, for most sports-minded people, the nation's most important cultural activity. New Zealand's international reputation began with the tour of 1905, when the team representing New Zealand acquired the name "All Blacks" and won every game in Great Britain except a still hotly debated match against a Welsh team, when a disputed try that would have established the complete supremacy of the All Blacks was disallowed. South Africa soon became New Zealand's traditional competitor for international supremacy in the game. New Zealanders now have cause to regret their blind devotion to sport, for it led in 1960 to a betrayal of one of the nation's proudest boasts. It has frequently been asserted that in New Zealand's biracial society Maori (the indigenous Polynesian) and *pakeha* (the descendant of Europeans) live in harmony and equality. Yet, even without a specific request from South Africa, the Rugby Union decided, against a considerable body of public opinion, to exclude Maoris from the team which was to tour the nation that practised *apartheid*. The clash of values implicit in such a decision is of far greater significance than some would admit. It demonstrated not only that New Zealanders were willing to put sports affairs before higher principles, but also that some aspects of their international activities throw light on the implementation of those values that are held in importance within the country. Fortunately, New Zealanders may still be proud of the present international repute of most of their athletes, because their

[1] *New Zealand's External Relations*, ed., T. C. Larkin (Wellington, 1962). This valuable book is an impressive record of the progress that New Zealand has made in the field of international relations, especially since the end of the war.

fame has not been won at the expense of other, more vital national concerns.

New Zealand Within the Commonwealth

Both in war and in sport, New Zealanders have shown that their greatest ties are with the members of the Commonwealth of Nations. Potentially, the most important tie is with Australia, a solidarity harking back to memories of "Anzac"—the Australia and New Zealand Army Corps who fought as one unit in the First World War. Even if this emotional force is beginning to fade, consciousness of a common regional, cultural, and historical background will continue to bind these nations to each other.

New Zealand was, during the second half of the nineteenth century, merely one of a number of Australasian colonies. Indeed, before 1840 she was part of the colony of New South Wales, which also administered Victoria (a separate colony after 1850) and Queensland (a separate colony after 1859). Van Diemen's Land (later renamed Tasmania) had been a separate colony since 1823. South Australia, founded in 1836, was colonized on principles similar to those which governed the founding of colonial settlements in New Zealand, thus creating a special affinity between them. Nevertheless, the commercial and trading connections with Hobart, Melbourne, and Sydney were the most powerful influences on the development of the colony of New Zealand.

From the very beginning, colonists in New Zealand thought of themselves as the equals or brothers of the colonists in Australia. The step-by-step evolution of all these colonies, and to a certain extent Cape Colony in South Africa, followed similar lines. Representative government was early accorded all of them and was swiftly succeeded by responsible government. Peregrinating colonists frequently had considerable experience in more than one colony—a most prominent example is that of Sir George Grey, who was Governor of South Australia (1841-45), of New Zealand (1845-53), and of Cape Colony before his second governorship of New Zealand (1861-68).

Friendly and very intimate relations of equality between New Zealand and Australia persisted after the Australian states achieved federation at the turn of the century. Many commentators see New

Zealand as a mere supporter (an active rather than a passive one) of Australian policies up to 1950, especially when these were in close harmony with the policies of Great Britain. The four self-governing states, or Dominions, within the British Empire had aligned themselves behind two rival concepts of their relationship to Great Britain. New Zealand firmly backed, and occasionally led, her closest neighbor, in opposition to the views of Canada and frequently South Africa. Essentially, the Australian-New Zealand concept was that of "Mother" England and her dutiful, grown-up, "British" daughters. But, in fact, New Zealand was always more obviously willing than Australia to leave policy decisions to the United Kingdom. New Zealand was the last Dominion to take advantage of the freedom of independent action conferred upon the Dominions by the Statute of Westminster of 1931. The Statute was adopted by New Zealand only in 1947 to enable the Government to carry out a purely domestic constitutional change. (It is interesting that this took place in the same year that independence was granted to India, Pakistan, and Ceylon.) This reluctance to cast off the legal ties of subordination even deprived New Zealand of official channels for conducting a foreign policy. In 1926, it had been agreed that all communications between self-governing members of the Commonwealth should be conducted government-to-government. Yet, New Zealand was still channeling all communications through the Governor-General (the representative of the Crown) as late as 1940. Despite this dependent attitude, New Zealand was always represented at top-level conferences and organizations and helped to mold the development of the extraordinary association of former British possessions now known as the Commonwealth. For quite some time, her independent voice was used to emphasize that it was the "British" Commonwealth.

Canada, with her French-speaking community, and South Africa, with her preponderance of Afrikaner colonists, could not, from the very beginning of their nationhood, accept the "British" concept, and their efforts to achieve equality of cultures within the framework of the evolving Commonwealth by resisting all attempts at centralization or "imperial federation" fortunately prevailed. It is doubtful whether New Zealanders are aware of the tremendous debt they owe to Canada and South Africa (no longer a member of the Commonwealth) for their present independence and self-conscious nationhood. The first purposeful colonizers of New Zealand set out from England in 1839—the year of the Durham Report, the first step in the development of responsible government for the Canadian colonies, and, ultimately, of the evolution of Empire into Commonwealth. The miracle of Canadian nation-building (coinciding with the first three decades of New Zealand's "colony of settlement") speeded, indirectly but powerfully, New Zealand's own constitutional development.

New Zealanders' feeling of comradeship and affinity with Canada has throughout their histories been somewhat attenuated by certain disagreements and divisive forces, but the solid ties that bind together all members of the Commonwealth are nevertheless present in great measure. The growth of the sterling bloc after the Second World War was probably the greatest barrier to the free exchange of people, capital, ideas, and material goods, for Canada was in the dollar area. The gradual dismantling of the sterling bloc has brought about closer relations, but New Zealand's rather Anglo-centric concept of the Commonwealth is at variance with Canada's fundamentally more sound Euro-Afro-Asian concept, as demonstrated in the Indo-Canadian entente that probably saved the Commonwealth during the Suez crisis in 1956. It must not be assumed, however, that New Zealanders are opposed to such a concept; it is perhaps fairer to say that they are just a little slow in adapting to "the winds of change." Although Australia accepted the Canadian concept of the Commonwealth's constitutional character during the Second World War, New Zealand's traditional respect for Great Britain's remarkable role has softened her own assertions of the essential equality of nations within the Commonwealth.

A sign of New Zealand's slowness in recognizing the inevitable passing of exuberant nineteenth-century British imperialism was the enthusiasm with which she participated in the South African War of 1899-1902. Relations between New Zealand and the Union of South Africa that developed a decade later were probably as close as, if not closer than, those with Canada. Despite misgivings about the racial doctrines that more and more came to the fore in South Africa, New Zealand made the Commonwealth doctrine of non-interference in the internal affairs of fellow nations a convenient reason for abstaining from criticism. When the question of race conflict in South Africa was brought up in the United Nations in 1955, only India and Pakistan voted against South Africa, and Australia, Canada, New Zealand, and the United Kingdom voted on the other side. But in 1958, Canada, Ceylon, Malaya, Ghana, India, Pakistan, and New Zealand voted against South Africa, with Australia and the United Kingdom opposed to them. On the question of the treatment of Indians in South Africa, Canada voted with India and Pakistan in 1955, and New Zealand, Australia, and the United Kingdom abstained. In 1958, New Zealand voted with the rest of the Commonwealth, leaving only Australia and the United Kingdom to abstain. New Zealand's sentiments about her own racial minorities are reflected in the vote. Pride in her principles of racial equality can thus cause her to vote against the two nations with which she has greatest affinities—Australia and the United Kingdom.

Though New Zealand does demonstrate a somewhat exaggerated respect for the British viewpoint, it should be noted that ever since the first Colonial Conference of 1887 her independent views have been voiced in Commonwealth councils. The Colonial Conference (renamed the Imperial Conference as of the conference of 1907 and now known as the Commonwealth Conference) has played a very important role in advancing the concept of freely associating sovereign nations, and New Zealand has always been an active participant.

A number of Commonwealth members are tied to India because a considerable percentage of their own citizens are of Indian origin. Just as Britain helped to create, by an immense flood of colonizers and other emigrants, a network of kinship ties throughout the world, so Indian emigrants also moved in great numbers to Africa, British America, Southeast Asia, and the Pacific. Because so many of these people moved into their adoptive homes as indentured laborers after the British abolished the African slave trade, their cultural influence has not been as pervasive as that of the British, but it has nonetheless brought particular problems and enrichment to a large number of Commonwealth countries, including New Zealand. In New Zealand, people of Indian derivation, along with Chinese New Zealanders, dominate truck farming especially in the retail trade. Such narrowly specialized economic activity tends to keep people of Indian descent isolated from the rest of the community and thus nullifies a great deal of their potential role as an important link between New Zealand and the modern states of India and Pakistan.

Differing viewpoints between Pakistan, India, and Ceylon, together with India's vigorous espousal of non-alignment, tended to keep Australia and New Zealand at a discreet diplomatic distance from these countries after 1947, but events during the past decade—especially the emergence of Malaya as an independent member of the Commonwealth and increasing Commonwealth cooperation in Southeast Asia—are bringing the Asian and Pacific members of the Commonwealth together.

When the Asian and African nations were added to the five "European" nations of the Commonwealth, New Zealanders tended to view themselves in the role of helping to make a multiracial community work in harmony and mutual understanding by bringing to bear their experience with developing their own successful biracial community. Relations with Malaya especially have given some cause to think that New Zealand may measure up to this ideal of good will, but much will have to be done within and without the nation before such a role can be taken seriously by other Commonwealth countries.

The emergency in Malaya caused by intensification in 1948 of Communist subversion brought a great deal of military, economic, and educational help from members of the Commonwealth, including New Zealand. After Malayan independence in 1957, New Zealand maintained an infantry battalion at Terendal, a small air force unit at Butterworth, and a frigate or cruiser for service in Malaya. Economic aid is perhaps most concretely represented by "Kampong New Zealand," a village built and maintained by New Zealand funds. The appointment in 1959 of a former Colonel of the Maori Battalion as New Zealand's High Commissioner to Malaya showed Malayans and New Zealanders alike how important a role distinguished Maori citizens are playing in creating strong ties with new multiracial nations of the Commonwealth. The signing of a trade agreement with Malaya in February 1961 demonstrated strongly the complete equality of New Zealand with Malaya and the other countries with which New Zealand has reciprocity agreements—the United Kingdom, Australia, and Canada.

Role in Aid Programs

The extraordinary growth of aid programs in the postwar period is such a distinctive characteristic of the times that future historians may well consider it to be the greatest contribution to world peace made in our time. Competition between the main power blocs to marry self-interest and self-protection by creating markets and relieving discontent in the "have-not" nations followed in the wake of postwar relief and rehabilitation programs for war-devastated countries. Such aid programs are most obviously obligatory for technologically advanced countries with a large volume of trade. New Zealand, despite its small size, is a major trading nation in the world, so it is not surprising that she too became interested in contributing to dissemination of technical skills, knowledge, and, to a certain extent, capital, among less fortunate nations.

Until 1950, New Zealand was passively involved in technical assistance programs of the United Nations through annual financial contributions and (slightly less passively) by providing some experts and training facilities. But in January 1950, at the meeting of Commonwealth Foreign Ministers in Colombo, New Zealand pledged her support for the bilateral government-to-government agreements for channeling aid; this has since been known as the Colombo Plan. By the middle of 1961, New Zealand had transferred nearly £7M.* in capital aid to a number of governments involved in the scheme, mainly by direct transfer of overseas funds but sometimes in the form of capital equipment. Over £2M. had also been spent on technical assistance, and over a thousand students had come to New Zealand. In 1961, 371 students were studying in New Zealand under the Plan, and 42 New Zealand experts were on assignment overseas, mainly in Asia.

When the Special Commonwealth Aid to Africa Plan (SCAAP) began in 1959, New Zealand pledged an annual grant of £100,000. Modeled on the Colombo Plan, SCAAP will ensure that African as well as Asian students will be able to study in New Zealand. It is still too early to see whether stronger links will be forged with Africa

* This would be equivalent to about $19.6M. (U.S.) at the present exchange rate of £1 to $2.80.

comparable with those now linking New Zealand with Southeast Asia. Both SCAAP and the Colombo Plan have resulted from Commonwealth cooperation, as has the Commonwealth Scholarship and Fellowship Plan, under which New Zealand offers each year ten postgraduate scholarships, three administrative fellowships, and three prestige fellowships for scholars of high academic standing. One hopes that very soon New Zealand, upon her own initiative, may make greater efforts to expand her education program to her nearest neighbors, the islands of Polynesia.

New Zealand's other aid programs are included in her obligations to the United Nations and to the Southeast Asia Treaty Organization. Altogether, about .15 per cent of New Zealand's national income (about .5 per cent of export income) goes into external aid programs. This is slightly lower than the contribution of Canada and Australia, and very much lower than that of the United States. There is still room for expansion, especially in fields where New Zealand experience is of special value. For instance, the pasture improvement and sheep husbandry project in Nepal, to which New Zealand has contributed a modest sum under the Colombo Plan, could well be built upon. Although her much larger contribution to factories in India and elsewhere for reconstituting dried milk has appealed to farmers looking for new markets for dairy produce, the more disinterested establishment of a faculty of agriculture at the University of Malaya or the projected one at a university in Northern Thailand create more good will. They not only serve as a concrete monument to New Zealand capital aid but also provide an opportunity for extending technical assistance from the store of experience gained in a century of farming and agricultural development. Projects combining capital aid, provision of New Zealand experts, and training in New Zealand of people from recipient countries to take over from the New Zealand experts in the new project have been found of greatest value, both in establishing a new project efficiently and in creating the maximum of good will between benefactor and beneficiary. The Delhi Milk Scheme (to which New Zealand has contributed £800,000) was fortunately developed in this spirit, with a maximum of attention to local needs and a minimum of attention to New Zealanders' hopes that Delhi's need for milk powder will create a market for her farmers.

(In fact, most milk powder is supplied by Australia.) This pilot project was followed by a dozen or so other schemes of a similar kind. Among other projects in which the three aspects of aid are efficiently combined are a civil service training center in Malaya and various technical training schools in Burma, Ceylon, the Philippines, and other Southeast Asian countries. Special training facilities established in New Zealand for Colombo Plan students also benefit New Zealanders. For instance, the experience learned in the English Language Institute in Wellington may be of great value in coping with problems in teaching Maoris and other people whose normal language is not English. At the risk of overemphasis, it is worth asserting again that it is certainly time that the lessons were extended to include education in the Pacific.

Trade

As might be expected, involvement with other countries is commonly dependent upon the volume of trade with those countries. It is therefore of considerable interest to see changing patterns in the destination of exports and the origin of imports. The United Kingdom has played the greatest part in New Zealand's twentieth-century trading patterns. Before the Second World War, 70-80 per cent of all New Zealand exports went to the United Kingdom, and about 50 per cent of her imports originated there. Exports to the United Kingdom since the war have gradually fallen to 50 per cent of the total; since 1959 less than half her total imports have come from the United Kingdom. Diversification of markets has reduced the dependence of New Zealand on Great Britain, but this tie is still the most important one in New Zealand's trading pattern.

Up to the 1870s, when the United Kingdom succeeded to the role, Australia was the major market for New Zealand exports. Within a decade, imports from the United Kingdom also exceeded imports from Australia. By the 1930s, imports from Australia were about 10 per cent of New Zealand's total imports, and exports to Australia about 4 per cent of total exports. The imbalance still exists and has recently been a sore point between the two countries. In 1961, about £11M. worth of exports were balanced against £47M. of imports. Negotiations on various levels have been conducted to redress this one-way emphasis and thus restore Australia as New Zealand's second most important trading tie.

Perhaps the biggest change in major trading patterns has been with the United States of America. Exports to that country in 1934, just as the world was coming out of the depression, accounted for but a minor percentage of New Zealand's total, and imports from the United States for less than 12 per cent of the total. By 1961, 14.40 per cent of New Zealand's exports were sent there and 9.41 per cent of her imports originated there. A similar change has occurred in trading with Japan. Exports to Japan in 1961 represented 5.22 per cent of the total, making Japan New Zealand's fourth largest customer. Imports from that country since the mid-1950s have steadily increased until in 1961 they represented 2.91 per cent of the total.

Trade with the European Economic Community in 1961 accounted for 15.63 per cent of exports and 8 per cent of imports. Canada has declined in relative importance as a destination for New Zealand's exports but in 1961 was still a major trading partner. Other major customers (those who in 1961 took more than £1M. of New Zealand's exports) are: Union of Soviet Socialist Republics, Czechoslovakia, China, Trinidad and Tobago, Jamaica, and Fiji (in that order); other major suppliers (those who in 1961 supplied more than £2M. of imports) are: India, Sweden, Ceylon, Switzerland, Netherlands Antilles, Hong Kong, and South Africa. (Those who supplied more than £1M. are: Malaya, Saudi Arabia, Singapore, Iran, Venezuela, Peru, and Indonesia.) New Zealand's strong ties with the Commonwealth are indicated by the fact that 59.3 per cent of her exports are to other Commonwealth countries, and 72.48 per cent of her imports come from those countries; nevertheless, a drop in percentage of exports taken by Commonwealth countries has been remarkably steady since 1953.

These figures indicate that New Zealand is gradually developing a broader international trading pattern and moving away from the ties of relatively free trade within the Commonwealth. Membership in the General Agreement on Tariffs and Trade is partly responsible, but determined attempts to diversify markets is accelerating the tendency.

Changes in New Zealand's diplomatic representation also reflect her trading patterns and her growing ties with other countries. In 1935, twenty-nine countries had representatives in New Zealand; by 1963, the number had increased to forty-four. In 1935, New Zealand's "honorary" government agents were to be found in Vancouver, Colombo, North China, Shanghai, Hong Kong, Johannesburg, Durban, Honolulu, and Fiji. Honorary tourist agents were posted in every state in Australia, in India, and in Singapore. A customs representative accredited to Canada and the United States of America was resident in New York. The British Chamber of Commerce in Marseilles had an honorary New Zealand representative attached; the office of New Zealand Trade and Tourist Commissioner in Europe (with headquarters in Belgium) was set up soon afterwards. The largest permanent establishment was the High Commissioner's Office in London. The second largest was that of the Tourist and Trade Commissoner for Australia. Smaller establishments headed by a trade and tourist commissioner were located in Toronto and Los Angeles.

In 1964, New Zealand was maintaining four ambassadorial establishments, in Washington, Paris, Bangkok, and Tokyo. The High Commissioner in Great Britain was also Ambassador to the European Economic Community, and consulates were maintained in Belgium, the Netherlands, and Switzerland. High commissioners represented New Zealand in Britain, Australia, Canada, India, and Malaya; the High Commissioner in India also acted as Ambassador to Nepal. The Ambassador in Bangkok was accredited to both Thailand and Laos; he was also New Zealand's Council Representative in the Southeast Asia Treaty Organization. New Zealand was represented in Indonesia by a chargé d'affaires and in Singapore by a commissioner. Trade commissioners had been appointed to Ghana, Hong Kong, Trinidad, and "the Pacific" (resident in Auckland). A trade correspondent was to be found in Tahiti, and honorary representatives of various kinds were resident in Argentina, Burma, Fiji, and South Africa.

International Organizations

The great change in external relations that is implied in these changes over the past thirty years is not wholly a product of New Zealand initiative. Before 1919, New Zealand did not have, nor did she wish to acquire, the right to exercise a foreign policy independent of the United Kingdom. She overzealously championed the cause of imperial federation in return for her right to protection from the British Navy. Membership in the League of Nations merely brought out the parsimoniousness of her small-nation mentality; suspicious fear of international labor and banking organizations underlined the fact that her government was farmer-dominated. (New Zealand refused to join the International Labour Organisation until 1935; until 1961 she refused to join such specialized agencies of the United Nations as the International Monetary Fund, the World Bank, and the International Finance Corporation.) After 1935, however, New Zealand became a vociferous advocate of collective security, and her representative (Mr. W. J. Jordan) frequently differed in public with Britain on matters of policy. Disturbing as this was to some of his countrymen, it marked the beginning of an integrity in international dealings that is a marked characteristic of public life within New Zealand.

The stubbornness and brashness of a tiny nation in sticking to principles in the prewar League was good practice for the considerable role that she was able to play in the creation of the United Nations. Peter Fraser left his mark on the San Francisco Conference, as a leading advocate of collective rather than regional security, of opposition to the veto, of increased power for the General Assembly (and thus for the smaller nations), and (no doubt ruefully, remembering New Zealand's checkered history in Samoa) of provisions for trusteeship and non-self-governing territories. New Zealand's record in the United Nations has not been brilliant; rather, it has been characterized by a somewhat passive earnestness and a reasonably consistent integrity. In standing by Britain over the Suez crisis, New Zealand showed that her unthinking loyalty to Britain could still outweigh her exercise of independent judgment, and a characteristic national caution more often than not leads her representative to side with the majority view of the power bloc to which she traditionally rather than regionally belongs.

Real New Zealand initiative in international affairs was to be seen only in the immediate prewar and postwar years, born of a rather naïve but laudable confidence in and longing for collective security.

Despite traditional distrust of measures for regional security, however, New Zealand followed Australia's lead in 1944 by signing the Canberra Agreement, a kind of watered-down Monroe Doctrine of the South Pacific. It paved the way for the ANZUS treaty of 1952, and for SEATO in 1955. One of the most promising outcomes of this new regionalist attitude was the creation of the South Pacific Commission, which held its first session in 1948. Britain, France, the Netherlands, the United States, Australia, and New Zealand—all of whom administered territory in the Pacific area—banded together to promote the well-being and advancement of Pacific islanders. The promise has not been wholly fulfilled, however, for although Australia at times shows considerable initiative, it is a constant irritation to some New Zealanders who really care about the future of Polynesia that their representatives do not. For instance, energetic drive and constructive thinking could be spent in reform of the South Pacific Commission, which, as an advisory body to the six governments, has not much power. Indeed, to most informed observers, the only really spirited international activity initiated by New Zealand since her immediate postwar effort has occurred when European trading nations have offered a threat to New Zealand's economic rights and privileges as an exporter of temperate-zone pastoral produce.

It is probably quite fair to assert that New Zealand fulfills creditably those obligations placed upon her by membership of established international organizations (including the rather ineffectual South Pacific Commission), but that she has not recognized on her own initiative the very considerable obligations placed upon her by her regional position.

One glance at a map of the Pacific should suggest that New Zealand, acting in accordance with her ties of kinship with Australia, must play a vigorous supporting role to Australia's leading one in Melanesia and Southeast Asia, that she must play at least an equal role in Antarctica, and that she must play a leading role (taking for granted some Australian and United States support) in the development of Polynesia. This last obligation seems especially compelling when one realizes that her third most important tie of kinship is with Polynesia. For among the two and a half million inhabitants of New Zealand, over 160,000 are wholly or partly Maori in ancestry, and more than 9,000 are Polynesian other than Maori.

The Tie with Polynesia

It is strange that the racial argument for New Zealand's special interest in Polynesia, which was a potent force in the nineteenth century, has not been revived until comparatively recently, under the influence of anthropological research. Angus Ross, in an article in *Anthropology in the South Seas* (ed. J. D. Freeman and W. R. Geddes), extracts the kinship aspect of relations between New Zealand and her Pacific neighbors[2] from his more general but unpublished work on New Zealand aspirations in the Pacific in the nineteenth century. Ross briefly mentions how in the early nineteenth century New Zealand became headquarters for Anglican missionary work in the South Pacific and how the Catholic and Wesleyan missionaries linked their island missions with New Zealand. He also briefly touches on traders' efforts to extend their frontiers into the South Pacific. He then goes on to stress how much more significant were the political schemes to secure the annexation of Fiji, Samoa, Tonga, and other island groups. Grandiosely promoted in England as "the Britain of the South" (a theme that still lures English migrants to her shores), New Zealand was intent on acting as the spearhead of a rather reluctant British imperialism in the South Pacific, claiming on-the-spot familiarity with European (i.e., French, and later Russian and German) imperialism as justification for her somewhat premature local imperialism. The racial argument in support of the usual economic and political arguments generally took the form of the claim that New Zealand should rule over all Polynesia because of her successful administration of the Maoris.

Ross accepts almost without question the truth of New Zealanders' claims to have evolved a native policy, after the civil wars of the 1860s, that was a cause for pride. He gives most of the credit to Sir Donald Maclean, who was Minister for Native Affairs from 1869 to 1876. But a cursory dip into the voluminous Maclean papers leads one to suspect that all was not as creditable as Ross would have us

[2] Other aspects will be found in Bernard K. Gordon's *New Zealand Becomes a Pacific Power* (Chicago, 1960).

believe.[3] Nevertheless, Ross's article provides very interesting insights into the political use of attempts to foster awareness of kinship ties among Polynesian peoples.

Sir George Grey, in *Mythology and Traditions of the New Zealanders* (*Ko nga Mahinga a nga Tupuna Maori* [London, 1854]), provided in written form a version of the oral myths of the Maori people which did much to preserve these myths during the breakdown of Maori culture that ensued in the seventies and eighties. Grey was also actively engaged in plans to use Maori kinship ties for the furtherance of British imperialism in the Pacific, specifically, to resist French expansionism, but such a visionary scheme could not be countenanced by the Colonial Office. William Seed's conversion of Julius Vogel to his project to annex Samoa in the seventies was also given only summary treatment, especially as Vogel extended it to include Fiji (whose Melanesian people seemed to him no different from Maoris). Maori members of Parliament, too, frequently employed reasons of kinship as arguments for New Zealand intervention in Samoa to protect the inhabitants from oppressive treatment by the Germans.

All these expressions of New Zealand imperialism culminated finally in a successful use of arguments of kinship and of experience in governing Maoris. In 1888, when Queen Makea Ariki petitioned the New Zealand government for British protection of Rarotonga from annexation by the French, she used the argument that Cook Islanders were of the same race as the Maori. A Maori Member of Parliament was among those in 1900 who advocated the annexation of the Cook Islands (including Niue) on the basis of kinship. Because most of the trade of these islands was with New Zealand, and because the British Resident from 1898 had had considerable legal experience among Maoris in New Zealand, British sanction for the annexation was forthcoming.

One of the considerations that played a large part in persuading Parliament was a stirring appeal to the example of Australia, which

[3] M. P. K. Sorrenson's "Land Purchase Methods and Their Effect on Maori Population, 1865-1901," *Journal of the Polynesian Society* (1956), provides disturbing detailed evidence that the complacent self-congratulation of New Zealand politicians was based on ignorance of the true state of Maori society and even of the settler-dominated policies of the governments of the day.

had at last achieved federation and was seemingly embarked on a policy of island expansionism. New Zealand had rejected—not very decisively—offers to join the federal Commonwealth of Australia. Henceforward, the two were to become friendly rivals in "colonial" imperialism. But the Cook Islands proved a big enough headache for an immature administration, and New Zealand's only decisive actions in the twentieth century were to help in expelling the Germans from Samoa in 1914 (Western Samoa was put under New Zealand mandate in 1919) and to take over administration of the Tokelau Islands officially from the United Kingdom in 1949, after having administered them in fact from 1925. New Zealand's record as an administrative power in the South Pacific has not been one to be proud of.[4] As there were signs, however, that a new understanding was being brought to bear in the year or two before independence was granted to Western Samoa in 1961, one may hope that New Zealand's role in her own hemisphere will not be hampered by her past ineptitudes.

[4] F. H. Corner, in his essay in *New Zealand's External Relations* (Wellington, 1962), dispassionately and carefully explains why.

TWO

FORCES FOR CHANGE

A brief survey of New Zealand's international affairs demonstrates clearly how very short is the history of her independence in dealing with the rest of the world. After a century and a quarter of European settlement, the modern citizen can look back only thirty years to the beginnings of an independent foreign policy. When he turns to internal affairs, he will find a comparably short history. The year 1935 (or perhaps a year or two earlier) marks a major watershed in the history of the nation. The hundred or more years of history before that date seem to most New Zealanders to be comparatively simple—deceptively so, as a new generation of historians is beginning to demonstrate. The history of the last thirty years, however, seems to be characterized by complexity and a bewildering rapidity of change in the whole character of society. The causes are only dimly perceived. It is becoming increasingly obvious that the purposeful transformation of the land by the pioneers into a far-flung pastoral province of Great Britain has had unexpected results. This realization is fostering widespread analysis of both historical and geographical causes of the present state of affairs, an interest that is being satisfied by a stream of scholarly and not-so-scholarly books. More such books and articles have appeared in the past two decades than in the whole of the previous hundred years.

It is nevertheless true to say that much of this interest has been concentrated upon detailed study of the early history of organized settlement. Thereafter, attention is confined mainly to political and economic history, with rather inadequate treatment of the last thirty years even in these fields. The best comprehensive history of New Zealand is probably still that of William Pember Reeves, which has been repeatedly revised and supplemented since 1898.[1] This book exuded a dignified confidence in the importance of New Zealand civilization to the developing British Empire. But a new trend in national attitudes was already developing before the book was published. An apparent loss of confidence in the peculiar destiny of New Zealand appeared to be occurring, a loss that may go hand in hand with an unconscious form of isolationism that still threatens to inhibit boldness and imagination in New Zealand.

This peculiar form of insularity seemed to overtake New Zealand about the beginning of the twentieth century. One cannot help attributing it to the effect of the real pioneering period of New Zealand—the opening up of small farms in difficult terrain that resulted from the establishment of a fixed market in Britain for refrigerated meat and dairy produce after the 1880s. For many decades thereafter, the people of New Zealand, led by a class of small farmers, occupied themselves with the task of creating a prosperous, well-organized, and highly productive country. The leaders of this effort were markedly devoted to principles of social justice, having inherited from earlier settlers a spirit of humanitarianism that was directed mainly at avoiding the inhumanity so typical of heavily industrialized Old World countries, and to a lesser extent the inhumanity of colonialism toward the native people of a New World country. Maoris willingly and laboriously helped in the process of breaking in the land; this was largely a result of the partial success of responsible government in solving the problems of culture contact between the irresistible aspirations of land-hungry colonists and the irrefutable rights of Maori landowners. That this immense struggle took place in a period of strong humanitarian movements in England was fortunate, but the greatest stimuli to maintaining this humanitarianism were undoubtedly the intelligence, courage, and adaptability of the native people with whom the colonists had to come to terms.

[1] The fourth edition, with additional chapters by A. J. Harrop, was published in 1950 under the original title *The Long White Cloud: Ao Tea Roa* (London).

The Coming of the Maoris

The arrival of the Maoris in New Zealand is still shrouded in conjecture.[2] Archaeological evidence has been accumulated for over a century, but the scientific or systematic study of it is a comparatively recent development. Two distinct cultures have been isolated: the Archaic (or "Moa-hunter," the more popular but less accurate term) and the Classic Maori (the pre-European culture flourishing at the time of European contact). The precise relationship between the two will remain unknown until a much clearer pattern is constructed from the archaeological evidence. Migration patterns of the Polynesian peoples are still hotly debated (even the precise linguistic relationships are in doubt), and migration patterns within New Zealand are largely theoretical. What reliable evidence there is suggests that a large number of Archaic communities were established in the thirteenth century along the eastern coast of New Zealand from Auckland to Murihiku. Many of those in the South Island lived on for centuries, and, indeed, a North Island community on an island in the Hauraki Gulf survived till the seventeenth century, surrounded on the mainland by a number of communities that seem to belong to the Classic Maori culture.

The sources of Classic Maori culture, both outside and within New Zealand, still have to be convincingly isolated and characterized. (Even a reference to the traditional homeland—Hawaiki—could produce in the 1860s an amazing number of explanations from Maoris, as a newspaper report of the trial of C. O. Davis, a *pakeha* friend of the Maori, demonstrated.) Despite some good work on the history of particular tribes,[3] migratory patterns, intertribal warfare, and tribal differences in material and non-material culture remain to be charted systematically.

[2] The best traditional account is to be found in the two books by Sir Peter Buck (Te Rangi Hiroa): *Vikings of the Sunrise* (New York, 1938) and *The Coming of the Maori* (Wellington, 1949). However, Andrew Sharp's *Ancient Voyagers in the Pacific* (Wellington, 1956) presents a fundamental reconsideration of traditional evidence.

[3] John Te H. Grace's *Tuwharetoa* (Wellington, 1959), or L. G. Kelly's *Tainui* (Wellington, 1949), are of most interest.

European Colonization

European colonization of New Zealand in the first half of the nine-teenth century was the result of two major pressures: the commercial extension of the Australian frontier and the purposive establishment of choice English colonies in accordance with a Utopian ideal of transferring to a country an anachronistic agricultural community undefiled by industrialism. As the Maori population was very un-evenly distributed over the two main islands, and as access to any particular region was almost solely by sea, simple generalizations (e.g., the traders came first, the missionaries next, and the colonizers last) cannot reasonably be made. Commercial imperialism (even including whaling and some sealing) was concentrated in coastal areas of considerable Maori population. Religious imperialism, al-though it throve first near trading centers, was perilously and hero-ically carried inland and overland and eventually enjoyed a pervasive influence throughout the whole country. Colonial imperialism was concentrated upon what land was readily and easily available, which frequently meant where there were few Maoris. Missionaries and traders, because of their intimate connections with the Maoris, tended to find themselves in opposition to English colonists in mat-ters of policy over land, colonial adminstration, and attitudes to the Maori people. A struggle between aboriginal protection and colonial aspiration in England was transferred with unequal balance to differ-ent parts of New Zealand, and thus initiated regional differences as hegemony shifted from region to region during the following century.

The major formative influences in New Zealand's subsequent history may be found in a number of good short histories, of which the most recent is W. H. Oliver's *The Story of New Zealand* (Lon-don, 1960). The best known is the textbook *A Short History of New Zealand* by J. B. Condliffe and W. T. G. Airy, now in its ninth edition (Christchurch, 1960). A close comparison of the various editions would provide an interesting historiographical study since 1925. The fact that Keith Sinclair's excellent book in the Pelican series, *A History of New Zealand* (Harmondsworth, 1959), has been called the Auckland history of New Zealand underlines the tendency in the past for regional viewpoints to influence the writing of histories.

Economic and Political Change

The emphasis placed by historians on economic history is probably to be explained by the overwhelming dedication of New Zealanders to maintaining prosperity and a high standard of living. This concern with material welfare, with economic security, is such a marked characteristic of New Zealand national attitudes that it may very well be the key to the cultural and social history of the country. But until cultural history develops into more than a survey of the national literature or of the visual arts, until social history rises above the unsystematic biographical or reminiscence level, until sociologists begin to take a very sharp look at both cultural and intellectual assumptions and aspirations—one cannot really be certain. For the present, however, it does seem true that a great deal of the history of the nation is grounded in its economic history.[4]

Seven periods in the economic history of New Zealand may be clearly distinguished. Each of these is directly linked with economic developments in the world outside New Zealand. In fact, New Zealand is so dependent for her prosperity on the state of the world market for her primary produce—meat, wool, butter, cheese—that it is impossible to consider her economic history in isolation.

The end of the first period conveniently coincides with a constitutional landmark, the Treaty of Waitangi and installation of a Governor, as well as with a socio-political landmark, the arrival of the first systematic colonizers in 1840. Before this time, sealers, whalers, and traders (from Tasmania, New South Wales, and from dozens of European and American countries) had established small settlements, many of them temporary, and most of which exhausted the very raw materials originally responsible for their establishment. New Zealand social history conveniently forgets the importance of these beachcombers and their somewhat more respectable followers, but a great

---

[4] The standard works are J. B. Condliffe's New Zealand in the Making (London, 1936 and 1959) and The Welfare State in New Zealand (London, 1959).

deal of trade developed in the period, especially after the institution of shore whaling in the late 1820s. The trading was, of course, two-way, and the experience gained by both Maori and *pakeha*-Maori (a European living with, and even like, a Maori) was to have considerable influence in the agricultural developments of the second and third periods.

The second period, roughly 1840-51, coincides fairly closely with the establishment of the six Wakefield settlements. The first contingent arrived at Petone (opposite present-day Wellington on Port Nicholson) on 22 January 1840; the last at Lyttelton (the port of present-day Christchurch) on 16 December 1850. Economically, the period was one of considerable hardship and disappointment, but these pioneers were preparing the way for New Zealand's economic boom after 1850. The second half of the 1840-51 period was somewhat more favorable than the first to agriculture and economic progress, especially as new settlements were mostly in the South Island.

The third period, roughly 1851-69, was characterized at first by vigorous economic growth. The golden metal, the golden fleece, and the golden grain were the immediate causes. The ultimate cause was the market established by the gold rushes. California in 1848 and New South Wales and Victoria in 1851 created favorable opportunities for the growth of the New Zealand economy, and the rushes that followed discovery of gold in Otago in 1861 brought still more people and capital and a lucrative local market for the Wakefield settlements. But in the North, Maori agriculture, which had flourished to supply the Australian market, suffered a setback due to falling prices in the late 50s and because of local civil war was unable to recover its previous efficiency. Depression hit the South hard by the late 60s; at the same time, the North was experiencing political, social, fiscal, and economic difficulties as the aftermath of punitive expeditions against so-called Maori "rebels." The division of New Zealand into two provinces of New Ulster and New Munster between 1846 and 1852 reflected a real cleavage in regional attitudes, and the six provinces created in 1852 merely overelaborated the division.

A fourth period, 1870-95, witnessed an optimistic investment boom followed by a long depression and a gradual recovery. In social, political, and cultural history (possibly even intellectual history, in a modest way) the period is perhaps more complex and exciting than all except the most recent. The abolition of provincial governments in 1876, inauguration of refrigerated cargo ships in 1881, and experimental social legislation introduced by the Liberal-Labour Party after 1891 are three major landmarks in the political, economic, and social development of the country.

The revolution in farming brought about by refrigeration coincided sufficiently with a period of rising prices in the world markets to ensure a steady prosperity for New Zealand in the fifth period, 1895-1920. Consequently, there was born an optimistic faith in the future prosperity of the Dominion (New Zealand had adopted this polite and dignified name in 1907) to supplement an exaggerated pride in its reputation as the "social laboratory of the world." This euphoric state of mind, encouraged by its farmers (the self-styled "backbone of the country"), ill-prepared New Zealanders for the violent economic fluctuations of the sixth period, 1921-34. The downward trend of world price levels boded ill for New Zealand's economy and caused considerable bewilderment and anxiety in the country. It is a great pity that the most detailed analysis of New Zealand's economic progress[5] stops at 1914, for this sixth period is probably the crucial one in the formation of modern New Zealand social and cultural attitudes. It is also a period that has not been sufficiently explored by general historians,[6] who are still attempting to rival the excellence of William Pember Reeves' earlier work.

The seventh and present period began in 1935 as New Zealand and the world were emerging from the Great Depression. For some New Zealand historians it marks the reassertion of the great movement of social amelioration of the 1890s, and even (for those who wish to pay homage to some dimly perceived cyclic pattern in the nation's history) a return to the true pattern of national development. It is also the period during which New Zealand's involvement with the

[5] C. G. F. Simkin's *The Instability of a Dependent Economy* (London, 1951).
[6] The best is possibly J. C. Beaglehole's *New Zealand: A Short History* (London, 1936).

outside world, as well as deliberate insulation from it, began to take shape. The development of the welfare state and the development of an international conscience side by side are two major facets of national development, and both were made possible by buoyant economic development during the period.

The seven periods thus defined by economic historians can be closely correlated with periods isolated by historians in other fields. Political historians tend to define periods since the introduction of responsible government in 1856 according to the accession to power of particular ministries, but their interpretation of parliamentary history is usually solidly grounded upon the conflict of economic interest so obvious in a rapidly developing economy. Social historians are well aware, in hailing 1891 and 1935 as significant points in the development of humanitarianism in New Zealand, that the distress of two great economic depressions preceded the periods so defined. Cultural historians tend to ignore economic trends, but their attempts to determine the precise point where a colonial literature or art became a national literature or art exhibit an aching desire to overcome the realities of a "dependent economy." Constitutional historians may define significant periods in the development of the nation's institutions, but constitutional developments, too, are a political manifestation of New Zealanders' attempts to grapple with economic realities. Indeed, all such endeavors to see meaningful patterns are profoundly affected by the facts of New Zealand's unusually narrow dependence on her pastoral industries and hence upon overseas markets.

The seven economic periods outlined above coincide clearly with economic cycles in world prices for primary temperate-zone produce. Up to 1935, in fact, New Zealand's internal development was almost entirely dependent upon the trends of economic development of industrial Britain. The seeming simplicity of New Zealand's short history before 1935 is a reflection of this simple relationship. The complexity and subtlety of her internal development since 1935 is the product of vigorous attempts to counter the worst effects of this unilateral but often profitable dependence, and the growth of mutual dependence has gradually brought about a more international outlook and a greater internal maturity.

Educational Change

As in most countries, the education system is a sensitive index of the community's ideals and sense of values and of the personal qualities of its citizens. The extent to which it embodies the social, political, economic, religious, moral, and intellectual ideals of the community is perhaps of lesser significance, however, than the extent to which it anticipates the needs of the community and influences and enriches that community through its products. In a country as small as New Zealand, it is possible to develop a high standard of uniformity but more difficult to develop diversity as well. Although New Zealanders have cause to be proud of the result of a century of national development in education, standards are not yet high enough for New Zealand's complex future.

No comprehensive history of education in New Zealand has been written since 1930, and no history of higher education since 1937.[7] Since the depression of the 1930s, fundamental and far-reaching changes have taken place, and are still taking place, so that a new history is unlikely to be written until present trends have created a stable new pattern. This period has evinced a marked rebellion against the tyranny of the external examination at all levels. The tyranny was perhaps world-wide in the nineteenth century, but its longevity in New Zealand was undoubtedly due to colonial desire to have local endeavor upgraded by non-local authority—whether or not the cachet thus sought was appropriate. Liberation from the need for external reassurance has led to a growing self-confidence in the educational values of the local systems. And gradually a new pattern is emerging.[8]

Characteristically, most education reforms in New Zealand have resulted from the investigations of government-appointed royal commissions that were created to satisfy strong pressure from interested

[7] Dr. A. G. Butcher's *Education in New Zealand* (Wellington, 1930), and Dr. J. C. Beaglehole, *The University of New Zealand: An Historical Study* (Wellington, 1937).

[8] The pattern can perhaps be dimly foreseen in two very important documents: the Parry Report (*The Report of the Committee on New Zealand Universities* [December, 1959]), and the Education Commission Report (more accurately, *Report of the Commission on Education in New Zealand* [July, 1962]).

sections of the community. Also characteristic, however, is the entirely unpredictable way in which their reports have been treated, irrespective of their intrinsic excellence or adequacy.

Educational theory and aspiration have kept abreast of modern developments elsewhere in the world since 1934, but the poor supply of adequately trained teachers has threatened to mar the practical application of theory. Such advances in theory have brought about fundamental changes in traditional teaching methods and in the structure of the primary school since 1936, and even more fundamental changes in the secondary school since 1945. A thorough overhaul of tertiary institutions seems to have begun in 1960.

In both scope and balance among the various subjects, the primary school curriculum in New Zealand corresponds very closely with that prescribed in Australia, Canada, the United Kingdom, and the United States. In the secondary schools, resemblances among the school systems of all these countries can also be pointed out, but local conditions have produced a distinctive balance of subjects, courses, and even methods of teaching. Tertiary institutions also have drawn on British, Australian, and American experience to produce a distinctive local form. In both secondary and tertiary stages, indeed, there can be no doubt that raising or changing of standards and complex diversification are proceeding apace. Educational developments are keeping up with the growth of economic diversity and changes in population. Whether it is keeping ahead is not certain.

When, in 1945, a reformed syllabus and examination system was introduced into the secondary schools, a new era of emphasis on social studies was inaugurated, in direct reaction to the stricter academic orientation of predepression days. A system of accrediting for entrance to the university helped to break the rigid shackles placed upon general education by a narrowly academic examination used to assess educational progress of all pupils. Pride in the success of the system in making New Zealanders more aware of creative, artistic, and humanist activities has been increasingly tempered in recent years by fears that it provides little incentive for pupils of high academic ability. Concern for the intellect of the brighter pupils is making very slow headway against complacent acceptance of the doctrine that education is primarily a preparation for unspecialized citizenship.

From the very first beginnings of the colony, New Zealanders have had a passionate regard for equality of opportunity in education. The doctrine has been stated again and again, but perhaps never so authoritatively as by Peter Fraser, Minister of Education, in 1939:

> The government's objective, broadly expressed, is that every person, whatever his level of academic ability, whether he be rich or poor, whether he live in town or country, has a right, as a citizen, to a free education of the kind for which he is best fitted and to the fullest extent of his powers.

This particular enunciation of the doctrine has been enshrined as a solemn ideal by the Commission on Education. It was not only the yardstick by which the commission measured actual achievement in education but also, in their opinion, "one of the dominant democratic ideas of the New Zealand community." One cannot help commenting, however, that the kind of education for which a particular person is best fitted and which develops his powers to the fullest extent is one that may produce a person not wanted or needed by the community. Or, a highly trained and educated person wanted or needed by the community may find that he cannot get in New Zealand the kind of education he is best fitted for. The phenomenon of the "export of brains" so common in the 1950s and before and the trust of New Zealanders in the overseas expert are the results.

Employment opportunity and educational opportunity go hand in hand. New Zealand's recent attempts to develop secondary industry, small though they may be, may well produce a sound effect on the growth of better values in the community. Without diversity of employment, secondary school education in particular cannot develop, and universities will always operate at a disadvantage.

Until very recently, the federal University of New Zealand practically monopolized tertiary education with its four constituent colleges at Dunedin (University of Otago), Christchurch (Canterbury University College), Auckland (Auckland University College), and Wellington (Victoria University College), and its two agricultural colleges at Lincoln (Canterbury Agricultural College) and Palmerston North (Massey Agricultural College). Powerful devolutionary forces transformed the constituent colleges into separate universities (two with branch colleges), so that on 1 January 1962 the University of New Zealand was no more. At the same time, other forces were at work to create a diversity of specialized tertiary institutions. From the polytechnic departments of certain technical secondary schools have evolved two regional technical institutes and the Central Institute of Technology. It is intended that the seven teachers' colleges at Auckland, Ardmore, Hamilton, Palmerston North, Wellington, Christchurch, and Dunedin will gradually be transformed into institutions of full tertiary standing. This process will be aided and possibly accelerated by the design and erection of buildings on an architectural plan embodying new concepts of teacher training. Some of the existing colleges will be housed in them, and three new colleges, near Auckland, in Wellington, and in Christchurch, will be added to the system within a decade. The whole of tertiary education is therefore in a state of complex modification. The success or failure of the vision of up-to-date tertiary education will be a severe test of what value the community itself places on higher education. It will soon be discovered what kind of society New Zealand wants and is willing to pay for, and just how conscious its leaders are of the role played by highly trained and liberally educated men and women.

Geography: Isolation and Local Power

The phenomenal growth of interest in cultural and social studies over the past three decades has fostered demands for explanation in historical terms of the present cultural and social life of New Zealand. It has also led to a greater awareness of the significance of New Zealand's geographical position. But it will be some decades yet before such awareness will compete with or predominate over historically determined assumptions about New Zealand's place in the world. Even the geographical fact that the country is at the center of an island-dotted, watery hemisphere is not yet part of the New Zealander's consciousness, and the logical conclusion—that some of the problems posed by such a fact must be recognized in order to be overcome—is still a concern of only a very small section of the community.

The New Zealander's awareness of geographical position is still un-consciously dominated by maps of the Pacific in which the upper and lower edges represent the polar regions and in which an aesthetic effect is provided by carefully balancing the land masses of the major continents, with Asia draped on the left edge and America on the right. To assess New Zealand's geographical isolation and peculiar position, a special map is needed, consisting of a circle with its center on Wellington, the capital city, and the circumference defining the true half of the globe in which New Zealand lies. It is then discovered that New Zealand's hemisphere gives no indication of the existence of huge land masses. North America lies over the "horizon," and from NNW to SE there is nothing but the tiny scattered islands of Mel-anesia, Micronesia, and Polynesia. To the SE near the horizon, over 5,000 miles away, lies the southern half of the west coast of South America, with the Straits of Magellan shielding the corresponding east coast; near the horizon to the NNW lies Japan. South Africa, India, Burma, all lie beyond the horizon. In the W to NW sector, at a distance of 5,000 miles, lies Southeast Asia and the Pacific coast of China, but these are shielded by the island continent of Australia, be-tween which and the Asian mainland lie Indonesia and other archi-pelagoes. The W to SSW sector is open expanse of ocean. And the remaining sector from SSW to SE is dominated by the centrally placed continent of Antarctica, the largest land mass in the hemi-sphere.

At the center of this watery hemisphere lie the two largest islands of Polynesia: the North Island (Te Aotearoa, or Te Ika a Maui) and the South Island (Te Wai Pounamu) of New Zealand. The Maori names are more descriptive than the English. Te Aotearoa (Land of the Long White Cloud) describes the North Island's appearance from the sea. It stretches five hundred miles from north to south, but its average width from west to east is less than one hundred miles. The shape of the island is better indicated by the other Maori name, which means the fish of Maui. Every New Zealander learns as part of the mythical history of his country the deeds of Maui-tikitiki-o-taranga, that redoubtable warrior, and more specifically of his use of the jawbone of his grandmother, Murirangawhenua. Among his ex-ploits was the great fishing trip during which he took his enchanted

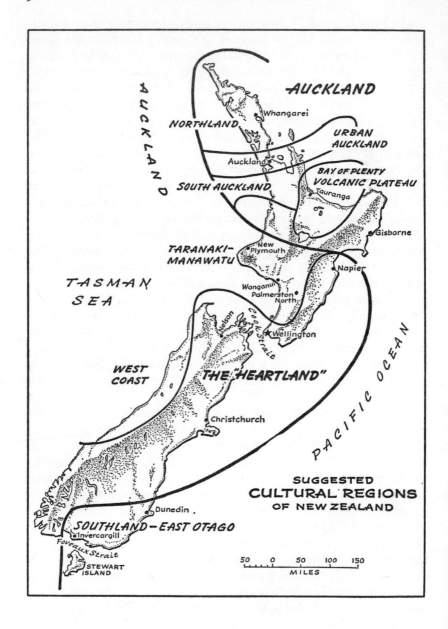

SUGGESTED
CULTURAL REGIONS
OF NEW ZEALAND

hook (pointed with part of the jawbone), baited it with blood from his own nose, and brought up from the depths of the ocean a portion of Papa-tu-anuku (the earth). Because Maui's brothers began cutting up the fish before he had reached the gods to appease them with a portion, the fish thrashed about briskly. Hence the mountainous nature of the island, and the distorted lineaments of the fish. Its twisted lower jaw forms Port Nicholson, upon which stands Wellington, the present capital city. The mountains that stretch northwest in broken ranges are the dorsal fins; Cape Egmont and East Cape (250 miles apart) are the tarsal fins. Lake Taupo in the center of the island is presumably a rather misplaced eye, and the long thin tail formed by the North Auckland peninsula has lashed out in a northwesterly direction instead of the predominantly northeasterly direction of the rest of New Zealand.

The South Island is sometimes called Te Waka o Maui (the Canoe of Maui) which suits South Islanders' sense of pride in being on the "mainland." However, the Ngatiporou tribe who live in the East Cape area of the North Island assert that the canoe is still atop Mount Hikurangi there. (Indeed, the enchanted hook now forms the Mahia peninsula). But Te Waipounamu (greenstone, or New Zealand jade) is a more common name for the South Island and describes it well. For the island, also five hundred miles long and about one hundred miles across, is like a slab of greenstone lying along a northeast-southwest axis. It is dominated by the dense green rain forests that cling to the sides of the Southern Alps that form an elevated spine close to the west coast. Most of the greenstone (nephrite) used for adzes or ornaments by the Maori people was originally collected on this west coast (Poutini) and was much prized.

New Zealand consists of these two main islands, a smaller one to the south (Stewart Island, or Rakiura) and a group of even smaller ones to the east of the South Island (the Chatham Islands). To the south and southeast are a number of isolated islands (only the most southern, Campbell Island, is inhabited), and to the northeast are the Kermadec Islands. All these, and a number of offshore islands around the coasts of the two main islands, constitute New Zealand proper. Administratively separate are her island territories (Tokelau

Islands, Cook Islands, and Niue Island), and, to the south, the Ross Dependency in the Antarctic.

The word "island," which recurs so often in this brief description, is the clue to the uniqueness of New Zealand as a New World frontier. Canada, the United States of America, South Africa, and Australia are all great land masses in which penetration of the interior dominated pioneering efforts. Communications by land or by river with the centers of Western civilization or its New World outposts brought men of a special "frontier" cast. But for nearly a century, New Zealanders' main links with civilization were by sea. The picturesque title of a book on the historical geography of the South Island, Andrew H. Clark's *The Invasion of New Zealand by People, Plants and Animals* (New Brunswick, N.J., 1949), suggests the uniqueness of New Zealand's development in comparison with that of other English-speaking New World democracies.

Overseas communications during the nineteenth century were complex, diverse, and surprisingly efficient. Locally owned (and frequently locally built) vessels plied a vigorous trade among the Pacific islands and between the Pacific coasts of America and Asia on a remarkably large scale. But improved long-distance shipping and other methods of long-distance communication inevitably destroyed this network. In the early twentieth century, the all-important trade routes between Europe and Australia and New Zealand came to dominate Pacific communications. Copra cutters, missionary schooners, and an occasional naval vessel are all that are left of the complex system of inter-island shipping that once connected the outlying islands with the main trade routes. The principal port in each group of islands is now visited by freighters at irregular intervals, and only a few (Suva, Apia, Papeete, Avarua, Vila, and Noumea) are served by regular freight, mail, or passenger ships. New Zealand itself is on only one major trade route, that between Australia and the Panama Canal. But only one Pacific island, Pitcairn, benefits from it, and most of Australia's trade goes westward through the Suez Canal. Fiji is on the second most important trade route, that between Australia and the Pacific coast of America, via Hawaii. In many ways it is actually a more important center than New Zealand for island commerce. New Zealand's ties with Fiji have been strengthened by air services (such as

TEAL's Coral Route) that link the main island groups with both Auckland and Nandi and also connect New Zealand with the other potentially important center that lies on a major route of South Pacific trade, Tahiti. Since 1961, shipping links with the Cook Islands have been greatly improved. The gradual improvement in communication throughout the Pacific is making it possible to encourage the economic and social development of islands in the South Pacific.

The external trade of New Zealand's island territories is almost entirely with New Zealand, because they lie in New Zealand's free trade area. New Zealand is currently exporting to other countries in the Pacific a mere 5 per cent of her total exports. Over 70 per cent of this amount goes to Australia, about 9 per cent to Hawaii and other American islands, another 7 per cent to Fiji, about 5 per cent to Western Samoa, and a little less than 2 per cent to Tonga. About 17 per cent of New Zealand's imports come from the Pacific (other than New Zealand's island territories), but Australia supplies nearly 99 per cent of this figure. The relatively minor imports from the islands are dominated by phosphate from Nauru, sugar and tropical fruits from Fiji, and tropical fruits from Western Samoa and elsewhere. Australia is a more vigorous trader than New Zealand, a fact that is far too casually taken for granted. New Zealand ought to improve her trade, and could certainly do so, by intelligently extending her current international aid programs to the South Pacific. Her major contributions so far have been in the fields of health and education. The Central Medical School in Suva and the number of New Zealand school teachers throughout the Pacific are visual reminders of this. But more technical assistance in agriculture and economic research is obviously needed, and the nature of her educational assistance needs thorough overhaul.

Polynesian Immigration

One particular advantage of stepping up aid to the islands of the South Pacific on the principles of the Colombo Plan is that large numbers of people from some of these islands have already emigrated to New Zealand. A vigorous policy of giving these people special educational opportunities would probably simplify the problem of providing experts for the Pacific islands and would make expenditure much more effective in bringing about economic and social advancement. New Zealand may well be on the threshold of a great new awakening to her international obligations.

Immigration of Polynesians is a postwar phenomenon of ever-increasing magnitude. Cook Islanders, Niue Islanders, and Tokelau Islanders are New Zealand citizens and may emigrate almost at will. (Permission must be obtained only from the local administration.) Western Samoans were New Zealand citizens up to 1961, but immigration was fairly strictly supervised after 1955. Tongans have always managed to preserve the independence of their kingdom, and as their thriving economy has enabled them to remain creditors of New Zealand, Queen Salote maintains control over emigration to a small community in Auckland. In 1956, there were 3,740 Samoans, 2,320 Cook Islanders, 917 Tongans, 848 Niueans, and 278 Polynesians from other island groups in New Zealand. The numbers since then have grown, until it is no exaggeration to say that the greatest migration in Polynesian history is now taking place.

This constant stream of immigrants is undoubtedly helping to enrich New Zealand urban life, but it also indicates a sad state of affairs in the islands themselves. Growth in population is double the world average, but the per capita volume of agricultural production has dropped during this century. Despite rather belated efforts to develop juice and fruit canning industries in conjunction with a government-sponsored scheme of planting and cropping on a complex capital investment system, economic development has been slow. In response to continual criticism, constitutional changes that will eventually lead to independence are now being made. Nevertheless, irresponsible and unthinking remarks by members of Parliament in debates on the present and future of the Cook Islands seem to be imbued more with the hope that the problem will soon be off New Zealand's hands than with the awareness that New Zealanders are responsible for the present state of unpreparedness and ought to be making some intelligent effort to improve the cumbersome agricultural scheme now being tried. Education (if it is merely basic education), health, and some necessary public works are not sufficient. Technical assistance based on fundamental research is the most crying need. The research now being done in New Zealand's other dependent territory, the Antarctic sector known as the Ross Dependency, is being carried on with admirable thoroughness and speed; unlike the South Pacific, Antarctica's development is not complicated by the needs of a rapidly growing population. Nevertheless, the possibility of discovering there some of the mineral resources so conspicuously absent in New Zealand, and other possibilities such as tourism and international airline flights over the Antarctic, make New Zealand's proximity to the area potentially very important. New Zealanders must look north with greater awareness and overcome that unconscious form of isolationism that threatens the country's future position in the world. When they do begin to pay proper attention to the islands, they will bring with them considerable experience of aid programs successfully carried out in Southeast Asia. They will also bring to such international activities many of the conscious and unconscious ways of thinking, feeling, and acting that they have learned in their struggle to create a new civilization in the South Pacific.

THREE

The National Character

Together let us beat this ample field,
Try what the open, what the covert yield;
The latent tracts, the giddy heights explore
Of all who blindly creep, or sightless soar;
Eye Nature's walks, shoot Folly as it flies,
And catch the Manners living as they rise.

Alexander Pope, *Essay on Man*, Epistle 1

Literature as an Approach to National Character

It is tempting to characterize the New Zealander by comparing him with his national symbol, the kiwi, that flightless bird, so well adapted to his own environment, shy, ungainly, yet whose habits are not fully known. Indeed, there have been many attempts to catch New Zealand's manners on the wing; when the captured bird is examined, it too often turns out to be New Zealand's folly, a dead duck rather than a live kiwi.

Nevertheless the hunt is worthwhile. The hunter of New Zealand's national characteristics has most frequently used as a starting point a preconceived notion of the national characteristics of Englishmen. According to his feelings about England, his analysis of New Zealand character is usually heavily laden either with deprecation of "colonial" habits or with well-meaning appreciation of "New World" habits. A modern Tacitus finds it extremely difficult to keep a cool head in such

38

circumstances, for he is comparing two parts of the same civilization and not, like Tacitus, analyzing a Germanic civilization largely unaffected by the habits and thinking of a Roman, a different kind of civilization. The psychological and sociological links between New Zealanders and Britons which make comparison difficult are nevertheless the links that make the comparison worthwhile. The subtlety of such links must inevitably make an analytical study inadequate, so it is not surprising that the most valuable comparisons are evoked in short story, poem, and novel.

A short story such as C. K. Stead's A Race Apart, for instance, or his poem Dialogue on a Northern Shore, suggest far more than the essays or books from which Desmond Stone constructed an anthology of comments on national character by visitors from overseas.[1] Nevertheless, Stone's handy little book is of considerable interest because it brings together from many sources (some of them difficult of access), lengthy quotations from twenty-one authors, from Samuel Butler in the 1860s to the French magazine Réalités in 1956. Nine English writers, one Scot, six Americans, two Frenchmen, one South African, one Canadian, and one Australian are represented. Some had lived in New Zealand for as much as a decade, but most had stayed for such a short time that their first impressions were not blurred by familiarity.

View from the Outside

Samuel Butler and Anthony Trollope, by virtue of their status as English writers, have long been enshrined in a special pantheon of interpreters of New Zealand life. Butler, in his amused but kindly comparisons of life in the Canterbury settlement with life in the England of his correspondents, distinguished many permanent characteristics of the national character.

> New Zealand seems far better adapted to develop and maintain in health the physical than the intellectual nature. The fact is, people here are busy making money; that is the inducement which led them to come in the first instance, and they show their sense by devoting their energies to the work. Yet, after all, it may be questioned whether the intellect is not as well schooled here as at home, though in a very

[1] *Verdict on New Zealand* (Wellington, 1959).

different manner. Men are as shrewd and sensible, as alive to the humorous, and as hard headed. Moreover, there is much nonsense in the old country from which people here are free. There is little conventionalism, little formality, and much liberality of sentiment; very little sectarianism, and, as a general rule, a healthy sensible tone in conversation, which I like much. But it does not do to speak about Johann Sebastian Bach's Fugues or pre-Raphaelite pictures.

Most of this holds true even today. It is also true of almost every new democracy. One may observe that perhaps the only peculiar characteristic of the Canterbury settlement which lingers in the memory from Butler's *A First Year in Canterbury Settlement* (London, 1863) is the pervading atmosphere of sheep and their effect on the transplanted Englishman's conversation, thinking, and interests. But one cannot help observing with wry approval that Butler carefully noted a tendency for colonials to turn into drunkards if they were not kept constantly occupied. Heavy drinking is still a national trait.

Trollope, by accident arriving in the far south in mid-winter, provided a tremendous fillip for the myth that New Zealand was really the Britain of the South. His comparisons with Australia and the United States stressed what is still true—that New Zealand seems more English than other former English colonies. His claim that New Zealanders outdid other colonials in blowing their own trumpets, especially in asserting that they were more English than any Englishman at home, is perhaps not quite so true any more. What trumpeting is now done is usually about the "superior standard of living." Perhaps Trollope's most penetrating comment was that the New Zealander, in imitating his brethren and ancestors at home, far surpassed his Australian rival in one activity: "He is very fond of getting drunk." Trollope also helped to popularize the half-truth that New Zealand was a paradise for servants, and he was the first distinguished commentator to note what many colonials felt then (and what many New Zealanders still feel)—that the country was overgoverned and overlegislated, and its parliamentary procedure bogged down in paper.

James Anthony Froude, the third of a list of eminent Victorian visitors, had little to say of national characteristics but a great deal to say of the possibilities which the natural features of the country seemed to promise for the growth of a national character. Visitors today, however, are struck more by the disparity between the variety and grandeur of the country and the monotonous sameness and smallness in the mental and moral stature of its inhabitants. Froude's description of Sir George Grey in his island paradise of Kawau may therefore be read as a description of a lost ideal of cultivated society in New Zealand.

Other distinguished writers occupy the pantheon of acceptable commentators because of their international fame (undoubtedly because the insecure colonial takes even the smallest crumb from their writings that will convince him that he has an identity). Although Mark Twain said some handsome things about the Maori, although Sir Alan Herbert packed a punch on the subject of tourism, although Bernard Shaw said a few commonplace things very wittily, the most illuminating comments have come from the writings of journalists, professors, and even, occasionally, diplomats. At the turn of the century, such men came specially to observe, for New Zealand had the reputation of being a "social laboratory." As Bernard Shaw himself said, after the Fabian Society had taken socialism off the barricades and made it an entirely respectable thing, it remained for William Pember Reeves to put the respectable program into practice not in England but in New Zealand. Thus, most of the commentators between Mark Twain and Sir Alan Herbert were intent on observing the New Zealander as a social humanitarian.

The American socialist Henry Demarest Lloyd, in his book *Newest England*, emphasized that New Zealanders, despite the weakening of the chain tying them to England, were just plain, everyday, matter-of-fact Englishmen who thought only of making a better living. He found that the most obvious characteristic (which he thought partly a product of climate) was a striking moderation in temper and politics. Thus, he hailed the "great strike" of 1890 as a New Zealand revolution in which moderate opinion was induced to perform a social right-about-face when the strike was ignominiously defeated. New Zealanders from then on led the world in the task of absorbing all classes into the middle class. So, for Lloyd, the characteristics of the English middle class became the national characteristics of New Zealand. Prosperity for all, no material want and no material splendor for anyone, became the nation's ideal. No Utopia was aimed at, because after a life of hard work its citizens still needed a state old-age pension.

André Siegfried, that acute French observer, still found a dormant Englishman under the noisy self-assertion of the New Zealander. At the same time, he found a constant battle going on within the individual between the colonial and the Englishman. English forms, he felt, were animated by a new spirit, and that spirit had grown independent of influence from America or other new countries. Siegfried's analysis of colonial attitudes is so sound and subtle that it would be temerity to try to sum it up here. Perhaps of greatest value, however, is the detailed way in which he explains the New Zealander's perfect mania for appealing to the state to protect him against any incipient growth of aristocracy, whether based on land, rank, or wealth. His judicious appraisal of the self-importance of New Zealanders, their sense of having a mission to humanity; his sympathetic treatment of the vanity and snobbery of this naïve, bustling nation; above all, his keen awareness of the reasons for its seemingly bold variations on English political and social traditions—all these make Siegfried still one of the best observers of national character. That he was French saved him from many of the blunders that an Englishman unconsciously makes in assessing the difference between the colonial and his parent country. That he had such considerable knowledge of other colonial settlements as well as European parent nations may be surprising in a man only thirty years of age, but what is more surprising is that his European predilections should have allowed so sympathetic an analysis of the predominantly middle-class, rather vulgar, and somewhat alien culture of an Anglo-Saxon colony.

James Bryce, Viscount Bryce, historian and diplomat, toured New Zealand in 1912. His somewhat superficial observations assumed special value, however, by being included in his *Modern Democracies* (London, 1921), in which the people and political institutions of six democracies—France, the United States, Switzerland, Canada, Australia, and New Zealand—are compared. Personal probity in public affairs, wide diffusion of education (except at the highest level), delight in outdoor activities, low ratio of thinking to talking, love of material comfort, complacency, humanitarianism, and many other qualities are noted. By avoiding direct comparison with England, something like a proper focus is possible.

Although interest in the national characteristics of New Zealanders up to the period of the First World War seemed to be prompted by curiosity as to the reasons for their "advanced," "socialistic," or "humanitarian" legislation, it must not be forgotten that comments were also frequent on the national propensity for drinking too heavily, ignoring theory and ideas in favor of common sense and practical action, worshiping the physical as distinct from the mental, and other signs of a colonial way of life emerging into a national one. But dissatisfaction with the faults in the New Zealand character and trenchant criticism of them have been a prime characteristic of the period since the depression, during which, it would seem, most people thought the nation "grew up," even if in a disappointing fashion.

When J. N. Findlay, in an essay in *Tomorrow*, expressed his exasperation with his adopted country, he gave utterance to a common attitude among New Zealand's intelligentsia in the late 1930s. He thought that an idealized vision of England—and a nineteenth-century England at that—was absorbing the emotional energies of New Zealand and keeping its inhabitants in a permanent state of feeble-mindedness and infantilism. This image of England, he thought, had lost its grip in other colonial countries but was perpetuated in New Zealand by a mindless obstructionism that tended to greet any effort toward change. Subsequently, he was to pinpoint the cause of this peculiar conservatism: a lack of confidence, an unnecessary caution on the part of the individual. The New Zealander is not only moderate and temperate (except in his drinking habits), as noted by earlier observers, but he is also modest. A strange alteration from Trollope's day! But, undoubtedly, Findlay is right. Modesty, or timidity leads to deprecation of, or even hostility to, criticism (critics are "moaners" and a nuisance); it also results in attempts to stifle eccentricity (even harmless eccentricity is unsettling) and an unhealthy fear of disturbing the status quo.

National sensitivity, which is remarkably close to touchiness, can best be judged from reactions to foreigners' adverse criticism. Expansive and open-minded American commentators are frequently surprised, even somewhat hurt, when their well-intentioned observations on New Zealand reveal how supersensitive New Zealanders are to criticism. Sydney Greenbie's eminently sensible and friendly article in *The Saturday Evening Post* of 1946 entitled "New Zealand's Uneasy Utopia" roused the ire of the Utopians so much that he abandoned plans to write a book on New Zealand. One has to be brave to write a book on the subject of New Zealand if it contains unpalatable truth. The most unpalatable comments in the article— that the New Zealander is a kind of middle-class Briton and a biologically standardized product of a British-oriented immigration policy— were undoubtedly true at the time. Moreover, Greenbie's comparison of what Americans and New Zealanders want out of life was extremely apt. But it was left to a former Englishman—now an American—Leslie Lipson, to probe more deeply into the differences between the United States and New Zealand. He analyzed them in terms of liberty and equality. In the U.S. the passion for liberty is often satisfied at the expense of equality; in New Zealand, the passion for equality often subordinates liberty to its requirements. But this glib summary does an injustice to the penetrating details that are to be discovered in his book[2] or even, for that matter, the short extracts in Stone's anthology. Such collateral comparisons are frequently more rewarding than a comparison between a parent community and its colony. But, unfortunately, nearly every comparison between the United States and New Zealand seems to emphasize shortcomings in New Zealand, so that local nationalism balks at learning lessons from the comparison.

Recent criticism of the New Zealand way of life has stressed the paradox between heroic activity overseas in war and increasing complacency and lethargy at home in peace, impoverished social life contrasted with easy material prosperity. And like many New Zealanders, strangers find the amount of restrictive legislation irksome and feel that it produces in its citizens a narrow attitude to personal liberty for the individual. Many impressionistic accounts like James Michener's are comically grotesque rather than informative, and others, like Eric Linklater's, tell us more about the author than about the subject of his

[2] *The Politics of Equality: New Zealand's Adventures in Democracy* (Chicago, 1948).

observation. After reading a number of such accounts, however, one must conclude that Linklater's attitude to the country is probably a common one—a curiously troubled affection. For despite the pervading air of bourgeois respectability, visitors quickly perceive that New Zealanders can be a vigorous and adventurous people.

A century of foreign observation thus leaves us with an impression of an easygoing, leisurely people, fond of outdoor sports and physical ease, who can be spurred into most impressive activity at need, who still have not learned to value intellectual pursuits and whose vigor has not made them keep up the pace of development toward an ideal that was so clearly perceived at the turn of the century, a people haunted still by some ill-considered myths about their relationship to a partly mythical England. It is an impression of a middle-class Briton whose bourgeois ideals have been modified by an equable climate and a trusting dependence on the state to keep his surroundings as pleasant as possible.

But a strident tone was introduced into discussion of the subject by the publication in 1960 of the most outspoken book to be devoted solely to an analysis of national characteristics—David Ausubel's *The Fern and the Tiki* (Sydney, 1960). Its carefully enunciated purpose was to suggest psychological reasons for a number of paradoxes about New Zealand behavior that struck its author when he came as an American Fulbright scholar to New Zealand for a year. He mentions New Zealanders' casual, almost lackadaisical attitude to life and their fervent belief in the value of stern discipline; the striking egalitarianism of adult social relations and the authoritarian atmosphere of secondary schools and universities; the nation's reputation for bold experiments in political democracy or social welfare legislation and its citizens' passion for safety and respectability; a strong trait of collective responsibility for individual well-being and a predominantly mid-Victorian social ideology emphasizing a punitive attitude toward personal inadequacy; condemnation of snobbery on the one hand and most peculiar manifestations of snobbery on the other; an elaborate system of academic, commercial, and trade qualifications and a pronounced lack of significant wage differentials for skill and hard work; uniformity of the predictably conservative newspapers despite independent ownership; relatively good racial relations despite a low level of public enlightenment on such matters; and above all, the laziness, inefficiency, and muddle of work habits contrasted with the tremendous energy, hard work, care, and effort put into sport and "do-it-yourself" occupations in the home.

Such kinds of paradox imply what Ausubel points to as the cause —authoritarianism in the training of young people. There is in fact a great deal of truth in his analysis of this and other causes of New Zealanders' more disagreeable national characteristics, and his plea for a liberalizing of the schools by an intelligent recognition of the shortcomings of disciplinarianism is a timely one. Nevertheless, his insistence on this ghost of the Victorian father figure as the major cause for latent repressed hostility beneath the New Zealanders' mild exterior is an oversimplification and seems, at least to sympathetic New Zealanders, to be a manifestation of what Lionel Trilling thought was so characteristically American about Kinsey. Ausubel has an impulse toward acceptance and liberation, a broad and generous desire that others (in his case, teen-agers) be not harshly judged. It would be unwise of New Zealanders to dismiss the book lightly or to ignore the generous impulse behind the prickliness of presentation, for it describes much shrewdly noted national behavior that is largely unrecognized by all except a small minority in the community. This minority has produced sounder and more balanced analyses of national behavior in such short articles as those by Bill Pearson or Robert Chapman in the New Zealand quarterly, *Landfall*, but we may still hope that *The Fern and the Tiki* marks the shaky beginnings of full-length sociological studies of New Zealand.

View from the Inside

It is interesting to turn from outsiders' views of national characteristics to views put forward by some of the most sensitive of the Dominion's poets and writers. Rather than offer a survey of the nation's literature, reference to a few volumes will serve both as an introduction to that literature and as documentary evidence that can bear the weight of sociological interpretation. The poem and short story by C. K. Stead which were mentioned earlier in this chapter, for instance, may be found in *Landfall Country*, edited by Charles Brasch (Christchurch, 1962), an anthology of some of the best writing published in *Landfall*, New Zealand's most distinguished cultural periodical. Stead's contributions may there be conveniently judged against other short stories (they reveal the high standard of New Zealand's contribution to the genre), other poems (the selection is of uneven quality), and a rather patchy collection of analytical and critical articles, the most valuable for our present purposes being Bill Pearson's "Fretful Sleepers."

In "Dialogue on a Northern Shore," Stead explores with great good humor and ironic self-knowledge the national attitudes and cultural misunderstandings of Englishman and New Zealander. The New Zealander is a modern Odysseus visiting an unidentified Greek island where the established values of Greek civilization are represented by an old man. The hospitable paternalism of the old man, his attempt to utter well-meant criticism, his fatherly irritation at what seems to him brash ignorance in the young are all contrasted with the urgent acquisitiveness, the laconic dogmatism, the uncivilized directness, the almost uncouth but meaningful impatience of the young man. When (in terms of the Penelope legend) our Odysseus attempts to explain why he visits the old country, the old man's patronizing attitudes are also contrasted with the unashamed arrogance and earnestness of the young man. The divergent meanings of the common English cultural tradition are amusingly symbolized by the two characters' opposite responses to the spirit who appears and sings to them. When Odysseus departs, after more misunderstandings, to complete his urgent pilgrimage, we are left with the impression that cultural and social values are very different but equally viable on both sides. The poem embodies many of the national characteristics of the New Zealander, but it exhibits sure signs that the idealized image of England is no longer sapping the emotional energies of the enlightened New Zealander.

Stead's capacity for detached, amused, yet trenchant observation is demonstrated in greater detail in "A Race Apart." The narrator of the story is a Mrs. Summerscroft, a woman brought up in the English middle-class tradition of wry self-analysis and slightly malicious social perception. Her lightly satirical treatment of the behavior of her English family is therefore appropriate as the expression both of her attitudes and of the author's. Andrew Nicholson, the New Zealander who takes the post of chauffeur to the family, is first presented to us through Mrs. Summerscroft's eyes, and her reaction is a mixture of pleasure and annoyance that might recall something of Eric Linklater's "curiously troubled affection" for Nicholson's country. English and New Zealand attitudes to menial occupations are first explored in a conversation replete with ironic implications. The humor of this part of the story is a result of delicate nuances of language achieved by insight into the characteristic use of the common tongue in both England and New Zealand. Nicholson makes a joke about his being the product of a rural community, and therefore one who likes to own things and one who is suspicious of governments in cities. The joke is a good example of the easygoing, self-deprecating consciousness of national identity common to many a modern New Zealander. The New Zealander's apparent classlessness is emphasized again and again by the narrator's comments on the strange habits of her chauffeur. The arrival of an American (automatically assigned by the Englishwoman to the same limbo, despite the great differences obvious to a member of a collateral democratic society) serves to emphasize the point even more.

But Nicholson is not strictly a member of the classless "middleclass Briton" type of society; he belongs to the only aristocracy in New Zealand, the physical élite. He is an athlete, modest about his abilities, but confident in his own way. He wins acceptance with the narrator's husband from his uncanny ability to judge horseflesh (picking winners is a prestigious occupation in New Zealand). English attitudes to the internationally acceptable sporting élite are amusingly sketched in with some current Balliol slang from a disgruntled member of the family, a touch of lyrical wonder from the narrator as she catches a glimpse of the runner in training, and excited colloquialism from the hero-worshiping girls.

The first peculiarity of the New Zealander observed by both the narrator and her creator is Nicholson's animal-like fear of decay and incipient death, symbolized by the diabetic and senile father of the narrator. (The young man in Stead's poem was repelled by the smell of age upon his landing in Ithaca's motherland.) The observation is linked with central themes in the story—purity and evil. These are introduced in a discussion on the thematic texture of Henry James's

Turn of the Screw; the discussion also introduces us to the American, Herman Parker, who is uneasy and apologetic where Nicholson is easy and detached. Nicholson's fear in the presence of physical sickness and decay, his defensive-aggressive assertions about his country and its high standard of living, his paradoxical condemnation of England and his pride in having experienced life in England, his frustrated efforts to verbalize his sense of national identity and separateness from England, all allow the Englishwoman to be slightly patronizing, and the American to bait him. His small-country disgust with "corruption" in older and bigger countries, his naïve idealism in the face of the American's observations upon evil and corruption, and his puritanical shock at the climax of the story emphasize a concept of the national character that stresses what Butler had already observed one hundred years before—that New Zealand seems far better adapted to develop and maintain in health the physical than the intellectual and emotional nature.

Analytical studies which consciously (and sometimes self-consciously) eschew the technique of comparison have also been produced by sensitive New Zealanders; one of the most important of these is Bill Pearson's "Fretful Sleepers," which is subtitled "A Sketch of New Zealand Behaviour and its Implication for the Artist." "Fretful Sleepers" was written in 1952; even in a decade much of the analysis of behavior has lost its relevance, although its truth at the time of writing was probably incontrovertible. Pearson's basic image of New Zealanders as intellectually and emotionally asleep, comforted by the dreams of security in equality and fretted by nightmares of the chaos and insecurity of reality, is, however, still fundamentally true to the facts of living in New Zealand. But new social pressures (and economic ones, too, for that matter) have begun to modify the kind of behavior, private and public, that unconsciously and often dishonestly aims at retaining the somnambulist status quo. The tremendous drive to prevent the development of "anti-social," non-conforming, original, or even eccentric individual talent in order to prevent disturbance of the dream is itself now under constant attack. Characteristically, the reason for this attack is to be found in a new form of the quest for security: unless New Zealand diversifies economically, her standard of living will suffer. Fear of losing material comfort is forcing the development of the kind of original thinker that a decade or two ago was suspect. Whether in the process of developing specialized scientists and social scientists a new kind of tolerance will be born is still a matter for speculation. Nevertheless, limited toleration for the development of relatively untrammeled individual talent has already occurred.

However, toleration of individual differences in behavior, thinking, and feeling is a sophisticated social phenomenon associated with urban life, or, more obviously, with metropolitan life. Such tolerance is notoriously linked with indifference. In Pearson's analysis, the hint of a special New Zealand variant of urban attitudes (shallow and sneering hedonism, a slicker and more hard-boiled set of attitudes) is detected in the South Islander's feeling of being uprooted when he comes to Auckland, where he senses the indifference and hostility of its people.

This urban-rural conflict has always been present in New Zealand, but no one seems to have questioned the assumption that the rural attitudes are the better ones. The development of urban and suburban life caused by increasing industrialization since the Second World War is a most remarkable phenomenon and will bring New Zealanders face to face with a new need to adapt. A particularly observant schoolteacher has pointed out that the only true city dwellers in New Zealand are in fact Maoris and islanders, who make up a great part of the central population of Auckland; most *pakehas* (non-Maoris) are victims of the myth that the true Maori is the rural one and that urbanized Maoris are uprooted Maoris. It is unlikely that Maoris are more aware than *pakehas* of the true values of urban society; but we shall return to such questions in later chapters.

Perhaps Pearson's most valuable contribution to the analysis of national characteristics is his careful assessment of the pressures of conformity on the sensitive and intelligent section of the community, who more often than not believe they escape from national characteristics by alienation. Because they are so few, they become a cult devoted to their own emancipation, a cult largely unaware of the number of attitudes they have retained from the community of which they no longer feel a part. Gossip is too frequently a substitute for an interest in ideas; scepticism that is otherwise healthy is misused to sneer at uncomfortable or disturbing ideas; the petty snobberies of the larger community are replaced by intellectual ones; the shallow poly-math replaces the practical man who can turn his hand to anything; and, because the community holds that being different is snobbery, the intellectual becomes a snob. An unhealthy scepticism is the only habit that the intellectuals do not share with the common man. In other words, the alienated intellectual is as much stultified by fight-ing against the community as he would have been if he had capitu-lated to it. The dilemma of the intellectual is described in several pages of urgent, heart-felt prose, and the solution is first hinted at, then suggested, and finally, with diffidence, carefully asserted. The artist must make a meaning out of the drives and behavior of com-mon people, take the very things that to non-New Zealanders are provincial and vulgar, and develop them to the point where they mean something to people outside New Zealand.

In his analysis of the drives and behavior of common people in New Zealand, Pearson has gone some way in preparing the ground for the artist to carry out these recommendations. Some of the points he makes about New Zealand behavior are very telling but need to be read in context for full understanding. Docile before authority, willing to persecute those who do not conform, afraid to accept responsibility, gullible in the face of headlines and radio pep talks, afraid of public opinion ("jury mentality"), two-faced toward social climbing, un-consciously assuming that morality is what others practice, dependent on second-hand, imported, and inferior culture, paralyzingly self-conscious, habitually predisposed to sneer, touchy, content with a life of "marking time," the New Zealander has never had such straight-from-the-shoulder criticism which is at the same time so sympathetic and understanding.

Ultimately, however, as Pearson is well aware, it is in fiction and not in analysis that national behavior is most completely captured. He himself has written a valuable appraisal of one aspect of the sub-ject: "Attitudes to the Maori in some Pakeha Fiction." [3] This was originally based upon *New Zealand Short Stories*, edited by D. M. Davin (London, 1953), an anthology which may profitably be read

[3] *Journal of the Polynesian Society* (September 1958).

in conjunction with *Landfall Country* by those wishing to know more of New Zealand literature and national characteristics.

Davin's selection of stories was frankly intended to throw light on the history of New Zealand, even though literary quality was his main criterion. Although the editor's introduction seems to be touched with characteristic New Zealand embarrassment at having to commit oneself to a choice, the two criteria of time and place are judiciously wielded. Certain periods and certain localities could not be represented because the editor lacked material of suitable quality, and certain short stories had to be excluded because the setting was already well represented. Of considerable interest to those seeking to define national characteristics is Davin's observation that the depression of the early thirties marked an important stage in the development of national sensibility. He very cautiously notes a seeming association between the gravity of the postdepression short story on the one hand and, on the other, a nostalgic quality, a return to the author's early life, a turning away from the present to the past. One might more dogmatically assert, however, that this is a contrast between the modern writer's self-conscious searching for an elusive truth and the confident wonder of the colonial optimist.

Indeed, one will find in postdepression short stories, poems, and novels evidence of the subtle social change that has modified a previously recognizable colonial sensibility.[4] Although poetry has flourished since the depression, the novel has only recently become an important genre in New Zealand literature. It would be impossible to select from the formidable number of novels a few that might be said to provide a comprehensive portrait of New Zealand society. But for a different reason it may be worthwhile pointing out Barry Crump's *A Good Keen Man* (Wellington, 1960). The phenomenal

[4] The poetry may be readily found in collections such as *An Anthology of New Zealand Verse*, ed. by Robert Chapman and Jonathan Bennett (London, 1956) or *The Penguin Book of New Zealand Verse*, ed. by Allen Curnow (Harmondsworth, 1960), both of which are prefaced by essays of sociological interest. The introduction to the second of these two anthologies especially is of such a quality that any attempt by a less-informed critic at a similar but shorter analysis is futile. For a lengthier treatment of the relationship between New Zealand literature and the tides of social change, the inquirer may consult E. H. McCormick's *Letters and Art in New Zealand* (Wellington, 1940) or the revised form of it, titled *New Zealand Literature: A Survey* (London, 1959).

success of this piece of fiction is undoubtedly due to the fact that a culture hero has been born. Perceptibly true to life, the lone deer culler is shrewdly self-reliant in the bush, mock-heroically scornful and ill at ease in the life of the towns, cynically and almost boorishly detached in all but one or two of his personal relationships, adept at keeping the welfare state (which pays him) at arm's length, disarmingly enthusiastic about the minutiae of his work, impatient and scornful of inexperience and incompetence, sardonically tolerant of other men's idiosyncrasies, and, above all, intolerant of any form of social or civilized life. He is in fact a projection of the New Zealander's dissatisfaction with the comfortable mediocrity and stultifying conformity he has created in his modern welfare state, a modern version of the myth of the indomitable pioneering spirit of earlier generations. Despite the laconic wit and the braggadocio naïveté, the hero is essentially an antisocial lone wolf, vigorously assuring himself that keenness in the work of his own choosing is the best way to keep the social, intellectual, and emotional world at bay. The comedy of the piece and the hero's naïve enthusiasm ensure that the reader admires this sophisticated representation of the narrowly materialistic figure of the dedicated pioneer. But the New Zealander who cares for some of the civilized values so churlishly and carelessly rejected cannot read it without mixed feelings. The book is, however, an engaging account of a pioneering era in the eradication of "noxious animals," and it reflects the New Zealander's joy in the untamed parts of his country.

If we return to postdepression short stories, we may find in anthologies something of this and of New Zealand's more sociable rituals and customs (Saturday night at the "pictures," race day, rugby football matches, picnics), and something of the tensions, feelings, and attitudes engendered in New Zealanders by their own social habitat. The one story that can be said to have caught the imagination of most New Zealanders above all others is Frank Sargeson's "The Making of a New Zealander." In it is concentrated the feelings of a generation of people who felt alienation within the country they had tried to conquer, a country they had transformed without themselves becoming an integral part of the country or even of its society. The transplanted Dalmatian is a more pitiable figure than a transplanted Englishman, for the Englishman, despite developments in his own country during the past century, still brings with him something of the social, moral, and spiritual values of the society from which New Zealand society stemmed. Nick the Dalmatian, who knew he wasn't a New Zealander yet but was no longer a Dalmatian, is the pathetic complement of the brash but isolated lone wolf in A Good Keen Man.

Frank Sargeson has an uncanny artistry in distilling the quintessence of New Zealand speech habits into his short stories. The New Zealander quickly detects the familiar accents of his own dialect of English in the dry, laconic style and recognizes in the brilliantly contrived rhetoric the distinctive rambling incoherence of his compatriots. Sargeson contrives to suggest the enormous depth of passion, feeling, and instinct beneath the surface of the prosaic "ordinary bloke," and he chooses as his vehicle the outcast from society, the casual worker, the shiftless hobo, the social failure or misfit, the men, women, and children who have rejected or been rejected by the smug respectability of suburbia. Thus, it would be grossly unfair and misleading to read Sargeson's stories as a report of typical New Zealand characters, even of the 1930s, or of typical behavior or typical mental or moral attitudes. A critical article by H. Winston Rhodes reprinted in Landfall Country should, however, help the non-New Zealander to identify the particular area of New Zealand experience which Sargeson explores. Although his short stories are not widely read and have not been reprinted for decades, he is the first writer of stature since Katherine Mansfield to delve deep into the roots of New Zealand malaise. His example has stimulated a host of short story writers since; for our purposes here it seems best to concentrate upon one of yet another generation.

The publication in 1959 of Maurice Shadbolt's sequence of stories The New Zealanders (Christchurch) focused new attention on the significance of the short story in New Zealand literary history. Behind the stories of people observed with compassion, insight, and humor lies a gentle but insistent message for the New Zealander. He must learn to accept his country, to come to grips with it, to appreciate the value of living in harmony with his natural surroundings. The landscape, the climate, those people who have won admiration for conquering the malaise of life in New Zealand, all point up the need for

acceptance and understanding, love and awareness of the unique conditions of life in the sun-drenched but temperate islands which make
up the country. To be a pale-skinned Polynesian instead of a sun-
tanned transplanted European seems to be the first step. The lesson
can be learned from the Maori who had already adapted to his physical surroundings before Europeans came and was subsequently able,
with enviable ability, to adapt to an alien culture. The figure of the
well-adjusted Maori often moves into the foreground of these stories
of maladjusted *pakehas*, but without sentimentality or illusion.

People well adjusted to their own country who appear in Shadbolt's stories are not only Maoris, of course, nor does he ever go too
far beyond his own experience by attempting to depict a Maori with
the same depth that he gives his narrators or protagonists. Perhaps
the most vividly captured figure is Isobel, the schoolteacher of Te
Waiotemarama, in the story "The Waters of the Moon." She lives
in Te Waiotcmarama because it is real to her, because the busy build-
ers (to borrow an image from the poet Denis Glover) failed to establish in the Far North their European-style civilization and therefore
left the area in peace and decay while they tried again further south.
A century during which the races and their separate ways of life have
mingled without an urgent attempt to force an alien culture on the
sleepy land has given her hope—and she speaks for many people in
the long peninsula north of Auckland—that in the future a new,
indigenous civilization may grow out of the ruins. This view of life is
bred from love for the country (or a part of it) to which she has given
her life and has resulted in a personality held up to us by her creator
for sympathetic admiration.

Shadbolt's gentle hints at the need for New Zealanders to adjust
through love and understanding to their natural environment is also
accompanied by only lightly veiled criticisms of some national attitudes that prevent the development of this adjustment. In "The
Woman's Story," for instance, there are superb descriptions of rural
behavior which allow expression of his resentment against English immigrants and "genteel" New Zealanders who perpetuate the myth
that life in New Zealand is second-rate in comparison with life in
England. The descriptions also allow pointed satire on those who
indulge in the snobbish anachronism of condemning miscegenation

or of misjudging through ignorance the values of Maori behavior and manners. And a characteristic resentment seems to obtrude surprisingly often: Shadbolt consistently but covertly attacks urban life because it appears to distort, corrupt, or siphon off the most promising signs of individual salvation. Living in close contact with the land in rural areas, it seems to him, has brought to individuals an appreciation of the desired civilization that is New Zealand's own and not someone else's. The attack on urban values is not unmitigated, however, for it is mingled with a great deal of careful observation, even loving observation, of people living their lives in New Zealand cities, usually Auckland or Wellington. The city may sometimes be portrayed as a dreamed-of refuge for those seeking to escape, but more often it is an alien environment which sharpens the conflict and makes the struggle more urgent, bringing the problems of life into harsher prominence.

It is with considerable interest, therefore, that one turns to the four stories in the first section ("Wave Walkers") of Shadbolt's book to observe how the author exposes the behavior of New Zealanders walking on waves felt throughout the world in our time. One wonders, nevertheless, how much Shadbolt's implicit advice contains the seeds of both benefit and harm to the New Zealander. On the one hand, it contains much to reinforce and justify the New Zealander's desire to develop and maintain in health the physical nature of his fellow citizens. On the other hand, it also seems to aim ultimately at helping to maintain in health the emotional and intellectual nature by making New Zealanders feel at home in their own environment—a largely rural environment, be it noted. A solid base in one's own rural culture and one's own landscape is a great help in releasing energies for dealing with universal emotional problems, but it is doubtful whether the problems of the intellectual health of the New Zealander are going to be solved by it. As T. S. Eliot pointed out in *Notes Towards the Definition of Culture* (London, 1948), friction between the parts of a society is necessary for the health of its culture. Shadbolt to a certain extent chronicles some of this friction that is developing in New Zealand and locates it in the city. His apparent hostility to the city must be taken as evidence of the vital growth of a rural-urban conflict (a subject which we will take up in the next chapter). Only when the quickened tempo of city life produces a love for the best of man-made things as distinct from our natural surroundings, an involvement with more than local affairs, and a sense of the value of urban culture as distinct from the predominantly suburban culture which now passes for both national and rural culture will such friction produce the proper environment for the development and maintenance of intellectual health.

```
┌─────────────────────────────────┐
│                                 │
│              FOUR               │
│                                 │
│           REGIONALISM           │
│                                 │
│                                 │
└─────────────────────────────────┘
```

The Australia–New Zealand Region

The visitor to New Zealand is often tempted to assert that
the way of life he finds there is very similar to life in Australia, the
only perceptible difference being a slightly "country cousin" atmosphere and a slightly slower tempo. Without doubt, New Zealanders
would deny the validity of such an assertion even more strongly than
Australians. In spite of this, there is a great deal of truth in the observation that the two countries are culturally very similar. The similarity
is often attributed to the fact that both are still merely distant provinces of England. Where provinciality or colonialism has been succeeded by new cultural patterns, the divergence between the patterns
in the two countries is then thought to be less than the divergence
from the parent culture. Observers of the differences between American and British ways of living frequently assert that what differences
there are in Australia and New Zealand may simply be summed up in
the statement that Australia is more "American" than New Zealand.
This attempt to define national differences in terms of the influence
of other countries is, of course, understandable in outsiders, for the
very subtle but important effect of local influences is often hidden
from the visitor. Unfortunately, it can also be hidden from the visitor's hosts if they are a people who have not yet developed a strong
tradition of intellectual reflection on their immediate surroundings. So
far, attempts to capture the flavor of life in Australia and New Zealand are to be found mainly in the serious imaginative literature of

the two countries, but no detailed comparison of the two literatures has yet been attempted.

Ever since New Zealand rejected the idea of joining the federation of Australia in the early years of this century, the possibility of some kind of political union has diminished. A sign of the times has been the gradual elimination during the past few decades of the word "Australasia" from the names of commercial enterprises and from books referring to both countries. The friendly rivalry between the two countries is demonstrated in exaggerated jokes common on both sides of the Tasman. The Australian professes to believe that New Zealand is some sort of appendage to Australia only just a little more foreign than Tasmania. (Indeed, Tasmanians are often said to be "very like" New Zealanders, an observation strongly influenced by geographical similarities between Tasmania and some parts of New Zealand.) New Zealanders respond with such comments as, "The distance between Auckland and Sydney is almost as great as that between London and Moscow; and the difference in attitudes is much greater." Even Australian regional jokes sometimes involve New Zealand. "Perth (in Western Australia) is just like a New Zealand city, and just as far from Australia." This kind of parochial joking stems partly from a desire to create feelings of regional identity and superiority, and partly from the actual existence of regional differences. The attempt to find similarities between ways of life in New Zealand and, say, Tasmania or Western Australia are vitiated by the undoubted truth that total national differences are probably greater than any similarities between separate regions of the two nations.

Perhaps a simple example will serve to illustrate. Australia and New Zealand both have a very sunny climate, so that in both countries the cult of outdoor sports, especially summer sports, has been developed to an extent unknown in England. The shorter working week made possible by high productivity in both countries has accordingly increased the desire to devote the weekends to amateur sport, with widespread participation. This phenomenon contrasts strongly with the primarily professional sports of England, where the spectator rather than the participant determines the pattern. The sporting sanctity of the weekend in New Zealand and Australia is an almost unconscious assumption of the new culture. But it has gone much further in

New Zealand than in Australia. Saturday and Sunday trading is much more strictly regulated, and a compensatory late shopping night on Fridays has been introduced. Because the shops are open until 9 P.M., suburban shoppers are able to come into the cities and rural shoppers into the towns. This has resulted in a nation-wide social phenomenon of beginning the weekend with a kind of carnival promenade around the brightly lit streets of the main shopping areas.

Australians visiting New Zealand are often surprised, amused, or delighted by the sight of young people dressed in their Friday and Saturday night best parading up and down the footpaths, greeting friends and acquaintances, flirting, staring at the jostling crowds, gossiping, and, sometimes, doing some shopping. Most New Zealanders are only dimly aware of their unique way of realizing the universal desire to mingle with one's fellow men and women.

In a city such as Auckland, one can see differences on a local level: unconscious class divisions may be detected in different blocks of the main street, Queen Street; then, when one walks along the other main street, Karangahape Road, a very different segment of society is seen. Queen Street is thronged with gay teen-agers and young married couples, mainly from outlying areas; Karangahape Road is full of family folk, often with children in tow, and the high proportion of islanders and Maoris indicates that they come from very near by, in the "inner city" area. The festive air and bustle are much the same, but the national custom is used to satisfy very different local needs. One is quick to notice, too, that the market day of Australian and New Zealand rural life, when compared with market day in England, has undergone a subtle change under the South Pacific sun. Friday night in the small towns, however, vies with market day in excitement and interest, especially for women and young people.

Most modern attempts to draw Australia and New Zealand together have helped to maintain close ties of friendship and common interest, have facilitated easy movement between the two countries, and have prevented any major misunderstanding. However, despite all exhortations to remember the Anzac spirit, despite rapid exchange of ideas from nation to nation, and despite increased solidarity brought about by improvement in communications and transport, the development of cultural differences will not be arrested. Australia's immigration patterns already show distinctive variations, and New Zealand's immigration patterns help to accentuate the difference. Recently, voices have been raised to advocate some kind of economic union between the two countries in imitation of the European Economic Union. It seems unlikely that economic cooperation will extend even so far as that practiced by members of the European Free Trade Area. Tentative negotiations have so far succeeded only in establishing the right climate of opinion for a common market agreement over forest products. The probably disastrous effects of open competition on the dairy industry of Australia or on the highly protected manufacturing industries of New Zealand make an extension of the principle into more than a few restricted fields a very dubious possibility. If an economic union seems a long way off, political union is merely a pipe dream.

Regionalism Within New Zealand

Within New Zealand itself, despite political and social unity, regional differences are being perpetuated and, in some areas, newly created. The existence of large numbers of Maoris in certain regions has left its impress upon *pakeha* cultural habits. The pride of *pakehas* in the Maori people, whether or not they are really familiar with the cultural habits of the Maori, is partly motivated by the feeling that they give New Zealand or areas of it a cultural distinction that Australia does not have. It is also partly due to the widespread belief that the Maori is superior to the Australian aborigine. The precise relationship between Maori and *pakeha* in different parts of the Dominion tends to affect New Zealanders' attitudes to racial problems elsewhere in the world, and variations in these attitudes are quite certainly a mark of cultural regionalism.

Systematic attempts to analyze regional differences in New Zealand are still in their infancy. Geographers are in the vanguard of those social scientists who interest themselves in the matter. Anthropologists have as yet only begun the task of charting the cultural diversity of Maori tribes. Dialect studies alone require a great deal more investigation. Detailed comparisons between material cultures must in the future be supplemented by sociological studies. Such cultural comparisons between regions should be possible in the not too distant future. General sociology, as distinct from social anthropology, has not yet attained its full status in the universities, so that sociological analysis of particular areas of New Zealand is likely to lag behind anthropological work.

Nevertheless, there have been a number of interesting attempts at defining the quality of experience in certain districts of New Zealand, and there are many signs of increasing interest in such matters, as for instance, in the pages of the quarterly *Landfall*.

Local history thrives in New Zealand, a reflection of strong provincial and parochial feeling. Largely amateur and unsystematic, it has frequently been confined to restricted topics such as ecclesiastical or military history or has been written to satisfy feelings of piety engendered by chronological commemorations, usually the centenary of the first *pakeha* settlement in the district. Social problems seemingly created by purely local conditions have drawn psychologists and other social scientists to make small-scale investigations into such practical studies as work patterns, industrial accident rates, and so on. A considerable expansion in postgraduate research in the universities is now under way, so there is reason to hope that particular investigations of this kind will soon be absorbed into a systematic study of cultural regionalism.

Geographic: The geographical regions of New Zealand have been analyzed with great care, notably in a series of Post-Primary School Bulletins issued between 1949 and 1953 by the School Publications Branch of the New Zealand Education Department. The results have been incorporated into a number of reliable regional geographies, the most detailed of which is K. B. Cumberland and J. W. Fox's *New Zealand: A Regional View* (Christchurch, 1958). In this, and in other books based upon the Bulletins, New Zealand is divided into eleven distinct regions on the basis of physical, biological, and cultural likenesses and differences. The most obvious physical difference is between the two major islands, so the five regions in the North Island (Northland–Coromandel, South Auckland, Volcanic Plateau, Taranaki–Manawatu, Eastland) are distinguished from the six in the South Island (Nelson–Marlborough, Westland, South Island High Country, Canterbury–North Otago, Southland–East Otago, and Fiordland–Stewart Island).

The Fiordland–Stewart Island region is extended to include the Southern Alps in regional geographies such as K. W. Robinson's *Australia, New Zealand, and the Southwest Pacific* (London, 1960). Culturally, the region thus defined is of some importance to the New Zealander, for "tramping," mountain climbing, skiing, exploring, deer stalking, and outdoor adventure are a cherished privilege to New Zealanders. As these remote, mountainous, unpopulated areas are many an urban-dweller's holiday dream, they have left a deep impression on the nation's literature and behavior. Within a few miles of the sea, mountain peaks rise to four, six, and eight thousand feet; the highest is over 12,000 feet and no more than thirty miles from the Tasman Sea. The Southern Alps were, so far as we know, the first sight of New Zealand to come to European eyes, for on 13 December 1642, Abel Janszoon Tasman reported seeing about noon *"een groot hooch verheven landt."* This ice-sculptured, high-lying land is clothed below the glacier-dotted tops with dense rain forest that makes the visitor recognize the claim that Fiordland is one of the wettest places in the world. This forest, or "bush" as it is called in New Zealand, shelters an enormous population of animals—red deer, chamois, thar, goats, wapiti, fallow deer, and even moose—and these are the main attraction for the rather transient population of the region. Even in this era of air transport, deer stalking and similar sports demand special qualities of endurance, adaptability, independence, and self-reliance. Mountaineering is both hazardous and exhilarating, for the rock is not as hard as in other alpine countries, and much climbing must be done on packed snow and wind-blown ice. It was not entirely an accident that the first men to climb Mt. Everest should be a Sherpa and a New Zealander.

The Fiordland–Stewart Island region provides an excellent opportunity to distinguish between a geographical and a cultural region. for the cultural value of this region is felt throughout the whole of the South Island, not just within the geographer's limits. The Southern Alps are a background to the activities of a very large proportion of South Islanders, and their influence is felt even unconsciously.

Stewart Island is culturally much less important for South Islanders, despite its inclusion in the same geographical region. Stewart

Island has perhaps a larger place in the culture of the Maoris. Fiord-land in the distant past was probably only a rather forbidding refuge for the Ngati Mamoe (the major tribe of Murihiku, the southern areas of the South Island); of more importance to them were the food-providing possibilities of the strait between Rakiura (Stewart Island) and the mainland. Oysters in the strait and mutton birds on the island remain an attraction for the Maori population of the Invercargill-Bluff area on the mainland even if freezing works and other *pakeha* industries are the main source of employment. The Maori population there is quite large in comparison with most other South Island areas, but not large enough to have had a distinctive influence on even the eating habits of the *pakeha!* Scottish traditions are certainly a much stronger influence.

It will be seen then, that although systematic regional geography may sometimes take into account cultural regionalism, it is much more concerned with physiographic, climatic, administrative and economic criteria.

Cultural: Perhaps the best way to define cultural regions is to ask the question, "Are there any people in New Zealand who can be distinguished from the average New Zealander by virtue of their regional origin?" Most New Zealanders would claim that a combination of geographic isolation and distinctive local history have left their mark on the South Islander, the West Coaster, the Taranaki "cow-cockie," and the citizens of the four main centers. Areas with romantic associations such as Central Otago, the Mackenzie Country, the King Country, the East Coast, and the Far North might also suggest to New Zealanders that there ought to be some kind of distinctiveness in people who come from these regions. The only cultural regions that might popularly be thought coterminous with those of the geographers would be Southland–East Otago and Westland. A single distinctive New Zealand "type" would be found throughout more than one of the geographers' regions, too. An example is the kind of sheep farmer usually thought of as belonging to the Hawkes Bay–Wairarapa–Marlborough–Canterbury areas.

Maori: If a Maori were to be asked what the distinctive regions of New Zealand were, his reply would be based upon his knowledge of Maori tribal structure. The East Coast region which seems so distinctive to *pakehas* is made so by a complex of related tribes, chief of them being the Ngati-porou. Many of the cultural traditions of the Ngati-porou have profound effects on the regional distinctiveness of Tai Rawhiti (East Coast). The King Country, too, owes its distinction to the role the various tribes there played in preserving some aspects of Maori culture from destruction. Tai Tokerau (Northland) also derives some of its cultural differences from the Maori tribes who live there. These regions, which the *pakeha* feel to be distinctive, are thus also distinctive for the Maori. But there are many other areas that appear culturally distinctive to the Maori that have not yet impressed their distinctiveness on the *pakeha*.

Sport: One other way of attempting to define a cultural area is to detect in individual New Zealanders loyalties to definite geographical regions. Winter sport is largely responsible for transforming what were originally administrative regions (within the old provincial system abolished in 1876) into cultural regions. Rugby football is the leading winter sport, and undoubtedly the national sport. Like most other national competitive games, it is organized on a completely amateur basis. Local clubs of players are linked to specific localities, schools or universities, or other institutions that provide suitable loyalty ties. District groupings lead to a national union, and players are thus provided with a ladder of achievement to encourage sporting endeavor. Chief goal of the club player is to represent his provincial association, especially in Ranfurly Shield matches. After that, success in reaching the New Zealand All Blacks team puts a player into the cultural élite of the country. The prestige of an All Black is supreme in a country where physical activity and bodily health is so highly prized. Other sports too, women's basketball and both men's and women's hockey, for example, are organized in much the same way and channel emotional loyalties into the old provincial boundaries.

Up till 1876, New Zealand was divided into nine provinces, each governed by a provincial council. They were Auckland, Taranaki, Wellington, and Hawkes Bay in the North Island, and Nelson, Marlborough, Westland, Canterbury, and Otago in the South Island. A tenth, Southland, had separated from, but was shortly afterwards reabsorbed by, the province of Otago. It would be a great mistake to overlook the strong provincial feelings that still remain in Southland as distinct from Otago. Despite fitful fluctuations in the strength of provincial feeling, provincial diversity had by 1876 developed to such a degree that the abolition of the provinces cannot be explained in terms of strong national feeling. Provinces that required much financial or economic help from the central government tended to be centralist; provinces that resented supporting less fortunate ones tended to be strongly parochial. Centralism was merely indigent provincialism. Variations in economic interests and in the system (or lack of system) by which they had been colonized created different forms of self-righteousness and different cultural assumptions in each province. Cultural regionalism had come to stay.

Administrative: When the central government in 1876 asserted the political unity of New Zealand by abolishing the squabbling provincial councils, it substituted a system of 63 counties and 36 boroughs with considerably diminished governing powers. Loyalty to the county has never been a strong cultural phenomenon, partly because the counties were gradually subdivided as population grew. They have remained primarily administrative entities. Loyalty to the town within the borough is, of course, very common. In 1908, town districts within counties were also constituted, so that when the 1961 census was taken, local administration was managed by 121 counties, 143 boroughs (including 15 cities), and 27 town districts. Town districts may be constituted if the population of a prescribed area exceeds five hundred; a borough may apply for city status when the population exceeds twenty thousand. Working in harmony (but frequently in disharmony) with this system of local administration is a proliferation of district boards: electric power boards, land drainage boards, rabbit boards, fire boards, harbor boards, hospital boards, road boards, and other kinds of service boards and authorities. In all, nearly a thousand local government authorities operate throughout New Zealand. The result is that a very large number of citizens are deeply involved in local affairs. Frequently, however, the old provincial ties continue to exercise their influence even through this maze of local authorities. The defining of more significant regions has in the past decade gradually become an official endeavor, largely as a result of the Town and Country Planning Act of 1953, which provides for the making and enforcing of regional and district planning schemes. Pride in one's region is an ever-developing source of New Zealanders' sense of identification.

Historical: Many regional characteristics may be traced back to a national or racial origin of the pioneers of the region. Yet many of the distinctive qualities in such racial or national groups have been completely swallowed by the dominant culture of the nation. The Bohemians of Puhoi, the Swiss or Poles of Taranaki, the Scandinavians of the Wairarapa, the French of Akaroa, the Germans of Nelson, even the Dalmatians of Henderson or Northland, are almost indistinguishable from the average New Zealander. But every now and again one is suddenly surprised by a non-British characteristic that emerges from the descendants of these European peoples. Scottish influence in the Far South or in settlements such as Waipu in the Far North is probably the most distinctive of all. Bagpipes, Highland games, curling, and a host of widespread Scottish activities provide evidence of the strength of Scottish refusal to forget their cultural distinctiveness. Domination of the Roman Catholic Church and its school system by people of Irish extraction perpetuates a peculiarly Irish flavor in many a New Zealand community, too. The mixture of Irish and Scottish characteristics is probably as obvious on the West Coast of the South Island as in any other region in New Zealand.

Distinctive Regions

One of the reasons for the distinctiveness of the West Coast is that the cultural region coincides with a special kind of geographical region. B. H. Farrell [1] has divided New Zealand into seven regions on the basis of its power resources (fuels, geothermal steam, hydroelectric resources, etc.). The only region where the energy resources dominate the life of the people is the West Coast, which also coincides with the regional geographer's Westland region. Farrell has in fact begun the task of dealing with regional geography on a specialized level that brings us closer in some cases to the culture of the region. Regional study of New Zealand will undoubtedly be enriched by other specialized studies in the next decade or two.

[1] *Power in New Zealand: A Geography of Energy Resources* (Wellington, 1962).

The Westland region is rapidly changing, for it is the only province of New Zealand where population is decreasing (about 33,000 at the 1961 census). Bill Pearson, the author of "Fretful Sleepers" mentioned in the previous chapter has captured a great deal of its cultural peculiarities in his novel *Coal Flat* (Auckland, 1963). This is in effect the first comprehensive attempt to write a regional novel in New Zealand. Other novels, notably those by Dan Davin and Helen Wilson, have been set in a cultural enclave of New Zealand, but none attempt to provide clear connections between the regional backgrounds of their characters and their behavior in a different regional setting. Some well-informed New Zealanders might quarrel with certain aspects of Pearson's analysis of regional characteristics, such as, for instance, the Taranaki background of the genteel schoolteacher, Miss Dane. Others may perhaps deplore some of the exaggerated descriptions of the behavior of members of certain social classes, such as the headmaster of the school. Nevertheless, anyone who has lived on the West Coast at the time in which the novel is set must grant that the author has captured the special qualities of that region. The novel has disturbed some critics in New Zealand, who would like to dismiss it as a "sociological" novel on the false assumption that such a novel is not "real" literature. Pearson seems to have carried out his own advice in "Fretful Sleepers"—to concentrate on the very things that English culture might call provincial and vulgar and to develop them to the point where they mean something to people outside New Zealand. His success may perhaps best be judged by the non-New Zealander.

The novel gives life to the assertion that coal mining has dominated the region ever since the gold fields that first brought settlement to Westland petered out. It would seem that sawmilling ought to be a more important industry, but large-scale exploitation of native timber only began (with much advertisement) in 1963. Westland is in fact a long, narrow strip of coast, covered by thick rain forest and dominated by alpine ranges that effectively separate it from the rest of the South Island. The unexploited forests are far to the south, away from the three roads and the single railway. The three ports are often unworkable because of the bars at the river mouths. It is no wonder that cultural distinctiveness has been preserved and that a romantic aura has gathered around the region. Like all areas opened up to settlement by gold seekers, the West Coast is littered with abandoned shacks and remains of ghost towns. It is becoming a great attraction for tourists dissatisfied with more accessible areas. The frequently lurid stories of the old days and the strong tradition of trade unionism among the coal miners give its inhabitants pride in their roughness, toughness, solidarity, and resistance to authority. In an aggressively egalitarian country, Westland exhibits both the aggression and the egalitarianism to a remarkable degree. Local myth stresses the peculiar warmth of hospitality that is to be found on "the Coast"; it is largely self-congratulation that inspires the myth, for such hospitality is extended most readily to those who conform to the rather narrow code of behavior expected of the inhabitants.

The other geographical region of the South Island that seems to correspond to a distinctive cultural region is that of Southland–East Otago, which has a population of nearly 300,000. One may be warned against overstressing the Scottish influences in this region by reading some of the novels alluded to above; Dan Davin writes of a little enclave of Southland Irish Catholicism in his *Cliffs of Fall* (London, 1945), and *Roads from Home* (London, 1949), and Helen Wilson writes of real Irish settlers in her book *Moonshine* (Wellington, 1944), which, though a literary failure, is a triumph of shrewd reporting. Southland–East Otago in many New Zealanders' minds is best summed up by the name "Hokonui"—that almost legendary, illicit whiskey distilled in the region, labeled with a skull and crossbones and secretively marketed with appropriate lyrical praise for its potency and excellence. Otago as a province is the only one to have received adequate treatment in a regional history—A. H. McLintock's *History of Otago* (Dunedin, 1949). Of the populated areas of New Zealand, Southland–East Otago is furthest from the main center of population at Auckland, nearly a thousand miles, in fact. It has the rawest, bleakest climate in New Zealand but is nevertheless fairly temperate by world standards. Although it is customary to treat with scant respect the phrase "the winterless North" as applied to Northland, the local pride and parochialism of the Scotland of the South has perhaps encouraged disparaging remarks about "the summerless South." A Scottish spirit of independence, a dogged determination to civilize a formidable but varied terrain and climate, have created a highly productive area devoted to all kinds of farming, timber milling, and mining. Its future, especially if aluminum smelting is established there, seems to promise some redress for the "drift to the North" which has been the major trend in modern New Zealand.

The Scottish characteristics of the inhabitants of the region (and of both Dunedin and Invercargill, its urban centers) are perhaps just as prominent "up Central"—in Central Otago, the southern section of the South Island High Country as delimited by geographers. Unlike the rest of the high country stretching northeast to Marlborough, Central Otago contains sheltered valleys where sunshine, low rainfall, warm summers, and irrigation water from the Clutha River have produced stone-fruit orchards and green pastures amid the rocks, mountains, and glaciated landscape. Schist predominates over greywacke and gives a distinctive beauty and awesomeness to the steeply sloped mountain ranges in the area. Like the West Coast, it was gold that brought a large population to Central Otago, but it was rugged individualism that kept those who remained after the gold fever was over. The Maori avoided it and favored Murihiku further south. Only the hardier sheepmen attempted to extend their labors to this area, and Scottish shepherds were among them. The language spoken in Southland and Central Otago is perhaps the only easily recognizable dialect of the New Zealand variety of English, and many of its distinctive characteristics can be traced to Scots.

The rest of the South Island High Country is devoted to sheep and hydroelectricity. It has been said that the only permanent communications between the region and other regions are the high-tension power lines. The natural tussock grassland has been grazed by millions and millions of sheep since the first squatters came in the middle of the nineteenth century. Station life here and in the pastoral areas of the Nelson–Marlborough region remains much the same as ever, despite changes in communications, and its similarities to station life in Australia make for very similar cultural habits. New Zealand literature and biography has been profoundly influenced by the fascination of such life, especially as it tends to have a socially distinctive aura about it; such "squattocracy" is New Zealand's equivalent of the Australian outback station, the North American ranch, or its South American variant. The photogenic quality of a high country mustering of sheep in the Mackenzie Country or Marlborough is continually being proved by the dozens of short feature films that are shown in cinemas throughout the English-speaking world.

Sheep were first pastured in the Marlborough section of the South Island High Country where it merges into the geographically distinctive Nelson–Marlborough region. This region is largely isolated from the rest of the South Island by the mountainous hinterland, and internal communication is rendered difficult by the alternation of northeasterly mountain extensions and strips of lowland. The largest of these lowlands enjoys more sunshine than any other part of New Zealand, and it is understandable why nine tenths of the population of the region is concentrated there, with Nelson the urban center. Further east is the less populous Wairau lowland, with Blenheim the urban center for much of the sheep country that surrounds it. Between these two lowlands the Marlborough Sounds highland terminates in a complex fiordland of great natural beauty and mild climate. Although geographically a single region, the two provinces are culturally somewhat different. Both represent very typically the tempo and attitudes of South Island life, but sunny Nelson, with its productive orchards, hop gardens, and tobacco farms, attract every year thousands of seasonal workers who wish to combine a holiday with some kind of financial assistance; Marlborough has the aura of New Zealand's premier sheep farming community.

The last of the geographers' South Island regions is Canterbury–North Otago, a region of lowland downs and plains, protected from excessive rainfall by the distant Southern Alps which form the backdrop to this coastal strip of about 250 miles. Here mixed crop-livestock farming is the characteristic occupation, and nowhere else in New Zealand are there vast areas so suitable for arable farming. Large sheep runs were first established in the region but gradually receded into the high country as bonanza wheat farming took over in response to the demands of the gold rush population further south and, later, on the West Coast. This brought about Canterbury's economic and political pre-eminence for a decade or two, but it impoverished the soil. New developments in the North Island (long delayed by problems over Maori land), the installation of refrigeration in ships to Great

Britain, the breaking up of large holdings of land, and other influences ushered in the present system of agriculture. Since its heyday in the 1890s (when one quarter of the nation's population lived there), the region has had a slow growth in population but a steady growth in intensification of farming, in productivity, and in agricultural diversity. Within this geographical region the influence of high country culture is still felt strongly, however.

Banks Peninsula, one of those many pockets of inaccessible country so typical of New Zealand, is much more like parts of the North Island than like the Canterbury–North Otago region to which it physically belongs. Although the French settlement which gave this charming area its characteristic place names might be thought to add to the distinctiveness of the area, there is little such cultural trace left. Nor have the Ngati-tahu, the Maori tribe for whom the rocky fastnesses— originally thickly forested—must have been an important refuge, left much of a mark upon present-day life. Christchurch holiday-makers from over the hills give the stamp of leisure and relaxation to rural communities whose farming patterns are similar to parts of the Eastland region of the North Island.

The region of the South Island that is most similar to the North Island is probably Nelson–Marlborough. Trade and traffic tie it to Wellington, and seasonal work brings many North Islanders there in the summer. Sea communication in the past linked the two New Zealand Company settlements at Nelson and Wellington, and similarity of outlook among the settlers was greater than between any two other early provincial colonies. It is, in fact, probable that culturally the South Island extends across the physical barrier of Cook Strait into at least the southern half of the geographers' Eastland region of the North Island. Establishment of sheep runs in the North Island began in the southern section and gradually spread north, with coastal shipping providing the main form of transport for men and flocks. This pastoralism took a different form from that of the South Island runs in that breeding rather than the production of fine wool became the chief aim. Merinos in the South Island in contrast to Romney flocks in the North are a visual reminder of this. But the way of life was essentially the same as that of the Australian sheep runs, and the local modifications do not disguise the cultural sim·

ilarity between South Island and Eastland region farming communities. Another link with the South Island is the unusual type of agricultural activity carried on amidst the sheep pasturing. Within the Eastland region more acres are devoted to special crops than in Nelson–Marlborough, and the pioneering quick-frozen vegetable industry is centered in Hawkes Bay.

Eastland (a geographer's term) is undoubtedly a homogeneous physical region, cut off as it is by a spine of mountain ranges mellifluously named Rimutaka, Tararua, Ruahine, Kaimanawa, Kaweka, Ahimanawa, Huiarau, and Raukumara. Nevertheless, the region has a certain amount of cultural diversity. Wellington–Hutt is an urban area physically isolated from its hinterland until very recent times; Wairarapa, Hawkes Bay, Poverty Bay, and the East Coast are names in common parlance that denote the existence of regional loyalties. The East Coast is the most distinctive of all, and it is made so by the Maoris. The Ngati-porou and other local tribes enthusiastically took up *pakeha* farming techniques early in the twentieth century and left their individual mark upon the social and cultural life of the farming communities. Nobody who has stayed in the region can forget the colorful panache with which they have transformed *pakeha* culture. "Color" is the right word. Piebald, skewbald, and white horses are preferred to the normal brown; shirts are brightly colored; broadbrimmed hats and waterproof clothing are worn with an air to be found nowhere else in New Zealand. Traditional Maori culture is prized, but so is the best in rural *pakeha* culture (in addition to special tastes like Hollywood Westerns). Inaccessibility is creating great problems of farm development and marketing, and the last dairy factory closed down in 1963 because farmers in the previous decade had increasingly turned to sheep rearing. Nevertheless, as one moves north up the Eastland coastal plains, the influence of the Maori seems to create a culture division that is more real than the physical division between North and South Island. North of Wairoa one in every three people is a Maori; south of Wairoa only one in thirty is a Maori, and in the county with the highest proportion of Maori inhabitants (Hawkes Bay County), the figure does not even reach one in seven.

A map showing those counties of New Zealand where Maori chil-

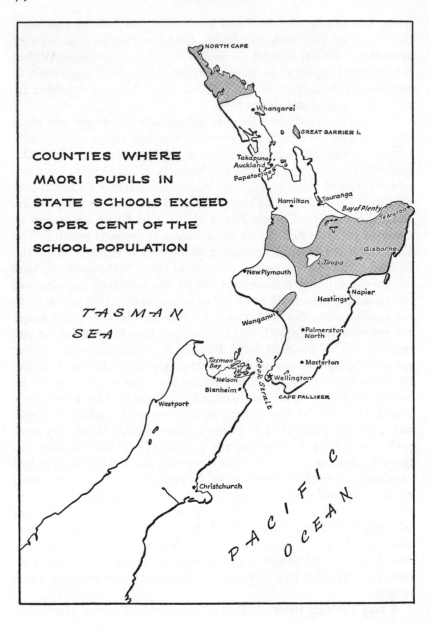

COUNTIES WHERE
MAORI PUPILS IN
STATE SCHOOLS EXCEED
30 PER CENT OF THE
SCHOOL POPULATION

dren in state schools form thirty per cent or more of the school population is probably the best indication of the extent to which Maori culture can be said to leaven *pakeha* culture. For, lacking precise sociological data, we must be content with likelihoods, not with demonstrable facts. Such a map shows a band across the middle of the North Island which in effect divides Auckland Province from the rest of New Zealand. Another concentration is to be found in the far northern tip of the province. The medial band stretches from the East Coast (where 90 per cent of the children are Maori) to Northern Taranaki (where 30 per cent of the children are Maori). The counties so distinguished are all exclusively rural, so that the predominant type of farming carried on in the area is probably the greatest determining factor in the cultural life of Maori and *pakeha* alike. Maps of the predominant type of farming suggest a further complication of cultural patterns. The sheep rearing Wanganui-Taranaki hinterland might lead one to conclude this area to be culturally similar to sheep rearing regions elsewhere. Like the East Coast, however, the differences caused by the presence of the Maori seem more pronounced. It is quite probable, too, that the Taranaki–Manawatu dairy farming regions, with their pattern of closer settlement, dominate to a considerable extent the cultural attitudes and activities of the hinterland and thus contribute to the feeling of difference rather than likeness. (See maps on page 172.)

Hazardous though such generalization is, one may perhaps affirm that a fairly homogeneous cultural region extends from the South Island (excluding Southland–East Otago and Westland) up the eastern half of the North Island as far as Wairoa. With some trepidation, one might also call this huge region the heartland region, for it bears something of the same relationship to the rest of New Zealand as the Midwest does to the United States of America. It has a population of about 800,000, and except for shearing gangs in some areas, and pockets of permanent Maori villages, the region has little or no Maori influence on its culture. In some parts of the North Island, it has obvious similarities with other regions south of Auckland Province, and in some parts of the South Island it shares characteristics with Southland–East Otago. But the all-important influence of sheep farming constitutes the most obvious unifying force in its culture.

It seems a remarkable coincidence that H. Guthrie-Smith's *Tutira: The Story of a New Zealand Sheep Station* (1921; 3rd ed.; Edinburgh, 1953) should deal with the area at the northern limit of this region. This New Zealand classic will give the uninformed reader profound insight into the roots of the culture in the region, and if read in conjunction with classics of South Island station life, should demonstrate whether it is permissible to assert or deny the homogeneity of the region. South Island classics such as Samuel Butler's *A First Year in Canterbury Settlement* (1863) or Lady Barker's *Station Life in New Zealand* (London, 1870) and *Station Amusements in New Zealand* (London, 1873) are possibly of greatest value.

In determining the national characteristics of the New Zealander, social scientists have consciously or unconsciously sought typicality among South Islanders or those who most resemble them in the North Island. It is not surprising, then, that the best sociological study of a community in New Zealand should be that of a rural community (350 square miles, population 1,800) in Canterbury. H. C. D. Somerset's *Littledene: A New Zealand Rural Community* (Wellington, 1938) is a perceptive study of a New Zealand equivalent of Middletown in America. If a similar study were to be undertaken of the same community twenty-five years later, it would still be typical of the dominant cultural pattern of the heartland region, but it would be much less typical of the rest of the North Island than the survey of the 1930s was.

The southern half of the western side of the North Island is the region to which another sociological essay, T. H. Scott's "From Emigrant to Native," seems to apply. The two articles so titled were printed in *Landfall* in 1947 and 1948 and are an interesting attempt to describe and discuss certain aspects of life in Te Whenua, a low country, dairy farming community equivalent to Littledene. The articles have a special value in that their author later went to live in the South Island, where he wrote "South Island Journal" (reprinted in *Landfall Country*) to explain his persistent feeling that he was living in quite a different country. The subtle distinctions are best read in context in the two essays, but we may point here to the growth in the inhabitants of Te Whenua of a very different view of history, tradition, and identity from those who live in the Old World or even in the heartland region of New Zealand. Scott describes in careful detail the foreshortening of history and limiting of geography that takes place in the minds of those for whom the pioneers were pastless men whose role was to introduce the present, and for whom the future is merely to be an improvement on the present. In such conditions, local feeling becomes a very potent force. The physical transformation of what was very recently bush-clad land or flax-covered coastal sand dune produces feelings about one's own identity and one's own hold on reality very different from those engendered by the seeming agelessness of the semicontinental South Island plain, downs, or high country.

The Taranaki "cow-cockie," or dairy farmer, is popularly thought to be a distinctive type in New Zealand, and a sociological study of the region may very well confirm the fact. But, lacking any reliable studies, we must turn to comic literature to see something of the stereotype. The personae of F. S. Anthony's *Me and Gus* (Wellington, 1938) probably fixed Taranaki types in the public mind. A modern version of 1951 (with two sequels) destroyed a great deal of the local color, however, so that "Me" and "Gus" have joined the ranks of the non-regional, comic "ordinary bloke." [2]

Urban Centers

Urban centers in the four broadly distinctive cultural regions we have so far discussed are intimately linked with the districts they serve and take a great deal of their cultural traits from them. There are notable exceptions to this generalization, however, for the word "urban" is a statistical, not a sociological, term, which may refer either to a borough or to a borough with city status. A "town," in common parlance, usually means what is technically a borough or town district. Culture in such towns is normally a mere sophistication of the culture of the country areas they serve. Although some cities demonstrate

---

[2] For those who want to dip into New Zealand's comic literature, J. C. Reid's *The Kiwi Laughs* (Wellington, 1961) is the only anthology that attempts to cover the field. Some regional humor emerges from it, not the least important of which is satire on regional myths and urban and rural behavior.

a specifically urban culture having very little connection with the surrounding country, most are still merely large towns with a population over 20,000.

Auckland Province is, on the whole, a cultural region distinctly different from the rest of New Zealand. Aucklanders are known to assert truculently that their province is superior to the rest of the Dominion in such jibes as, "The South Island really begins at 39° S." The parochial sentiment contained in this half-truth is designed mainly to infuriate Wellingtonians, whose regional pride is frequently expressed by derogatory remarks about Auckland. This urban rivalry is probably a greater source of cultural diversity than any other form of regionalism. Before we deal with the cultural pattern of Auckland Province, therefore, we must look to urban differences.

Until a decade or two ago, New Zealanders frequently read advertisements by firms which boasted branches "in the four main centers"— i.e., Auckland, Wellington, Christchurch, and Dunedin. Although these still constitute the main urban centers of population (in 1961 they included over two fifths of the population) there has been a steady increase in the significance of other urban centers with city status. In twenty years, the population of Invercargill, for instance, has risen from 30 per cent of that of Dunedin to 40 per cent. The highest rate of population growth has recently been in Tauranga, Rotorua, and Hamilton, all in Auckland Province (which passed the million mark in 1961). The largest absolute numerical growth of any urban area is in Auckland, which has been adding between 10,000 and 15,000 people to its population every year during the past decade. Indeed, the increase in the Auckland urban area (Auckland city, Takapuna city, and associated boroughs) is greater than the combined absolute increase of population in Wellington (including the Hutt urban area), Christchurch, and Dunedin. The Auckland urban area now includes almost one third of the urban population of New Zealand, and almost one fifth of the total population. Coupled with the fact that Dunedin (the most distant of "the four main centers") has the slowest urban rate of growth, it would seem that Auckland is fast becoming *the* urban center of New Zealand. But census figures do not tell the whole truth. Auckland is situated on an isthmus, and both to the north and to the south there is plenty of flat land, albeit dotted with extinct volcanic cones and overlooked by the Waitakere and Hunua hills. This means that the inhabitants have been able to convert the area into a vast series of suburbs with local allegiances and cultural differences of their own, so that the metropolitan area is in fact relatively small. It is frequently remarked that "Wellington is more of a city than Auckland," because the smaller population of Wellington is concentrated into a smaller area. It also has the advantage of being the political capital of the nation and of being administered almost entirely by the Wellington City Council. Only a quarter of the inhabitants of the Auckland urban area live in the Auckland City Council administrative area, and the whole sprawling conurbation is divided into about twenty boroughs, two cities, and many other local authorities. The movement to create an over-all metropolitan administration has not yet resulted in any satisfactory organization. In 1963 it seemed likely that four cities would emerge: North Shore (north of the Waitemata harbor), Waitakere (west of the Waitemata and north of the Manukau harbor), Auckland (south of the Waitemata and west of the Tamaki River), and a South Auckland city covering a 250 square mile area south of the other three cities. But parochialism may prevent even this development; the traditions of local government are strong in New Zealand.

Despite the gradual breakdown in the concept of "the four main centers," the stereotype of the kind of person who lives in these cities is still distinctive, and it is commonly linked in popular assumptions with the precise origins of the original settlement.

The Aucklander is supposed to be brash, breezy, and rather boastful—in keeping with the commercial and capitalistic nature of the present-day city and with its commercial origins. It was founded in 1841 as the intended capital of the colony, but Commerce, in the shape of Brown, Campbell, & Co., was already established on an island in the Waitemata harbor. When officialdom arrived in Auckland, commercial entrepreneurs and speculators were already seeking their fortune in the new capital. For decades, even after the capital was transferred to Wellington in 1865, Auckland was thought to be more Australian than any other town in New Zealand and much more commercial and aggressively opportunist than the carefully planned settlements further south. It was, in fact, the frontier town of Australian traders and merchant adventurers.

Wellingtonians are supposed to be much smoother characters than Aucklanders, more metropolitan, and wise in the tricky business of administration of government power and the workings of the civil service. Their suavity of manner is thought to be in keeping with their closeness to the corridors of power and with the self-conscious gentility of the New Zealand Company pioneers. For Wellington was the first of Edward Gibbon Wakefield's attempts at "systematic colonization." Of course, the kind of society that did develop in the Company's settlements was quite different from what had been envisaged. But the settlers brought with them expectations that forced them into vigorous opposition to both the settlement and the government on the shores of the Waitemata. Commercial entrepreneurs in Auckland, who were wholly dependent upon trade with the Maori, were not very sympathetic to land-hungry settlers. The government, too, was imbued with the spirit of humanitarianism that had prompted the Treaty of Waitangi. It considered that the Maori must be protected from the depredations of "land sharks." The bone of contention was the Crown monopoly of the purchase of Maori lands for resale to settlers. The New Zealand Company was not interested in protecting Maoris; it was interested in protecting British migrants. The beginnings of provincial rivalry (and the later urban rivalry) may thus be traced to a conflict in England—between the humanitarians of the missionary societies, who had learned from earlier colonial experience the fate of primitive peoples in a new colony, and the systematic colonizers, with their eyes on the miseries and difficulties of English society about them.

Urban rivalry between Auckland and Wellington is perhaps greater than between any of the other main centers, but southern resentment against the northern cities is understandable when it is realized that Dunedin was the largest city in New Zealand until 1881 and that Christchurch was probably the most important city in New Zealand during the last two decades of the nineteenth century. Indeed, the South Island was "the mainland" until 1901; most people lived there, and *pakeha* civilization there was much more advanced.

Remembrance of the past importance of the South Island lingers in the rather self-conscious retention of the term "mainlander" in semi-jocular parlance. (North Islanders are dubbed "Pig Islanders" because Captain Cook liberated pigs there.)

The stereotype of the Christchurch inhabitant is genteel, Anglican, cultured, and decorously conservative. He is thought to be more English than the English and to inhabit an illusory world of colonial gentry, in keeping with the cultural pretensions of the Canterbury "squattocracy" for whom the city is the urban center, and in keeping with the origins of the Canterbury settlement. The predominantly pastoral hinterland was settled by systematic colonizers under the leadership of John Robert Godley, whose very name seems to sum up the pretensions of a city whose focus is a cathedral with strong English associations.

In contrast, the Dunedinite is stereotyped as a slightly mellowed Scot—tough, resilient, canny, and stoutly respectful of learning. His cold, rather bleak, and orderly city, with its stern Victorian façades, reveals its past commercial importance, probity, and industry, and both inhabitants and their city are thought to reflect the determined spirit of its pioneers. It was religious schism that prompted the Scots to come to Otago and to plant a moral, pious, and industrious settlement free from the acrimony of a disrupted Presbyterian Church.

None of these stereotypes is, of course, an accurate picture of any citizen of the four main centers, but they nevertheless exert an influence upon the cultural habits of the metropolitan populations of New Zealand. New Zealand's education system is heavily indebted to the Dunedinite's respect for learning and to Otago experiments in local education schemes. Christchurch, strengthened by the heartland of which it was early the political, social, and economic center, has no doubt helped to prolong—for good or ill—New Zealand's ties with England. Wellington, from its physically isolated but geographically central position, has developed a civil service and an administrative system of which New Zealand may well be proud, and its inhabitants, until recent times cooped up within the hollow of the hills surrounding their superb harbor, have evolved a true urban culture where the intimate exchange of ideas is facilitated and a national spirit fostered. Auckland's raw commercialism and vigorous economic complexity has played a unique role in the development of pugnacity, individuality, and self-criticism in the New Zealander, a constant source of irritation to the rest of New Zealand.

What is the likely future role of the four cities and their citizens? Dunedin may very well continue on its traditional canny way, with its eyes turned largely on the region which, a fanciful Southlander has said, is marked off from the rest of New Zealand by a tartan curtain along the Waitaki River, but if large-scale industry comes to Invercargill, a revolutionary vitality may be released as old ties with Australia are new-forged. Christchurch, with its increasing manufacturing and industrial strength, its international airport, and its role as headquarters for "Operation Deep-Freeze," may well produce an urban society more outward-looking—and southward-looking—than it has in the past. As yet, the significance of Antarctica has not penetrated public awareness, but it may do so within a very short time. Wellington will, as its administrative classes become increasingly rich in experience and knowledge, undoubtedly act as a conservative curb on the centrifugal forces at work in other regions. Auckland will need this curbing, for there can be no doubt that it is still essentially a frontier town. Despite increasing sophistication in worldly ways, Aucklanders are deeply divided by petty parochialism, by brash antagonisms between dimly defined social classes, by cultural friction caused by diversity of racial and regionalist groups, and by a restlessness of spirit not found elsewhere in New Zealand. Frontier preoccupation with the making of money, frontier spirit of enterprise, frontier scorn for non-practical intellect, and frontier habits of looking toward new horizons are still part and parcel of living in Auckland.

The vast number of suburban areas in Auckland nevertheless hinders the development of a specifically metropolitan tone of life in the city. As in all major cities, the population of the inner city has declined steadily as large office buildings are built on the sites of the old one-storied and two-storied buildings of an earlier period. In 1961 the population was 17,194; in 1936, 37,055. Suburban life is being gradually eliminated from the center, and the true urban population is changing rapidly in composition. What is most spectacular is the fact that in the four central areas (Freeman's Bay, Auckland Central,

Newton, and Grafton) the Maori population has increased enormously. In 1926, one person in every 101 was a Maori; in 1936, one in 58; in 1945, one in 16; in 1951 and 1956, one in 12; and in 1961, one in every 8. In 1956, one in every 20 was a Polynesian other than Maori, one in every 64 was Chinese, and one in every 167 was Indian. The numbers of non-Europeans in 1961 are not yet known, and even 1956 census figures do not indicate the undoubted diversity of nationality in the European population. Nevertheless, these figures should be sufficient to indicate how truly cosmopolitan and varied is the inner city area of Auckland. Many of the people who live in the area are semitransient (e.g., university students, people in state flats waiting for a suburban home to become available). A strange and exciting mixture of rural, suburban, and city life pervades the area, but the unique combination is fast changing as semislums, charming old houses, and not-so-charming shops are replaced by motorways and blocks of offices and flats, university buildings, and new shopping facilities. Vitalizing cultural frictions are nowhere in New Zealand more obvious, which makes it certainly true, as the Minister for Maori Affairs noted, that Auckland will be the crucible of the future in race relations. It may also be true that out of the melting pot will come a specifically New Zealand form of that higher culture which Eliot describes in his *Notes Towards the Definition of Culture*. Because Auckland has by far the greatest number of Polynesians and a significantly large percentage of all the Asians in New Zealand, her citizens are likely to take an increasingly large part in initiating New Zealand's involvement in Pacific and Southeast Asian affairs.

Urban Auckland's cultural frictions are to a great extent an intensification of those to be found throughout Auckland Province, whose most obvious ties are with Manawatu–Taranaki. Geographers tend to include Northern Taranaki in this region, but culturally it is part of the King Country, which is in many ways most like the East Coast. Geographers distinguish three other regions: North Auckland–Coromandel, South Auckland, and the Volcanic Plateau. The most highly concentrated economic development in the past decade or two has taken place in these regions. In the southern suburbs of Auckland is concentrated the largest industrial and manufacturing complex in New Zealand; it is fast changing the decentralization of industry that has hitherto been characteristic of the nation. A little further south, centered on Pukekohe, is a multiracial agricultural community that has some cultural affinities with two similar communities in the Manawatu–Taranaki region.[3] Of all multiracial societies in New Zealand, these bear watching most closely, for they represent a rural antithesis to the racial crucible of the city and seem to generate more prejudice than any urban community.

Further south, centered on Hamilton, are the rich dairy farming regions of the Waikato and Hauraki plains, mainly *pakeha*-owned, exhibiting what might be called a quintessence of Manawatu–Taranaki cultural habits. The cultural similarity is not quite as strong as the economic similarity would lead one to believe, however, for the strident regional loyalties of the people of Hamilton smack a little of rural resentment against urban Auckland, a resentment taking its tone from Auckland as Hamilton attempts to compete with it culturally. Centered on Ngaruawahia, twelve miles north of Hamilton, is an increasingly important cultural regionalism of a special kind. Turangawaewae *marae* is the center of the Maori King Movement, which originated as a nationalist movement to protect Maoris from losing their land to *pakeha* settlers, but which has since developed wide cultural functions. Its influence is most obvious during the Coronation celebrations in October, when Maoris (and some *pakehas*) throughout the countryside take part in competitive sports, traditional cultural activities, and serious or not-so-serious discussions. The force of Maori culture is thus becoming increasingly felt in those areas which were unjustly wrested from the Waikato–Maniapoto people a hundred years ago.

Further east, the Bay of Plenty region shares to a large extent the cultural attitudes of the Waikato, but modifications are likely to be felt as a result of the profound influence of the multiracial societies evolving on the Volcanic Plateau which forms its hinterland. Hydroelectric dams built on the Waikato and Rangitaiki rivers were the

[3] One of these was the subject of the sociological study by Ernest and Pearl Beaglehole called *Some Modern Maoris* (Wellington, 1946).

projects that first brought together in a single-industry settlement
a complex multiracial community. Of these, Mangakino was from
1947 to 1961 the largest; its population reached nearly 6,000. It is a
great pity that no one has attempted a detailed sociological history
of this remarkable community so that regional differences might be
determined by comparison with W. J. Campbell's *Hydrotown* (Dunedin, 1957), a revealing study of a Central Otago equivalent. Joan
Metge's "The Human Factor," a lecture published in the New Zealand Geographical Society's collection of lectures entitled *New Zealand's Industrial Potential* (ed. by R. G. and M. W. Ward, Auckland,
1960), goes some way toward providing such a survey and has the advantage of also describing the effect of the large forest industry town
of Kawerau on the life of other inhabitants of the area. The forest industries are developing permanent new societies of a kind unknown
in New Zealand before the last decade, and they, like Auckland, may
also be a crucible of the future. Exploitation of geothermal areas is
also creating a changing pattern of life on the Volcanic Plateau.

The northernmost of the geographers' eleven regions is North
Auckland–Coromandel. Most Aucklanders would affirm that Coromandel has been culturally distinct from Northland since sea transport ceased to be the dominant unifying force in the province. Strong
historical associations in the North give its inhabitants their sense of
regional distinction, and it is the only region in New Zealand to pub-
lish a specifically regional magazine devoted to its culture. Much of
the quality and distinctiveness of living in this primarily pastoral region dominated by the sea may be deduced from this unpretentious
little periodical, *Northland*. Perhaps it might remind us of those
snatches of conversation in Shadbolt's "Waters of the Moon" between a teacher involved in the culture of the region and a journalist
recuperating from a malaise that includes expatriation. The myth by
which the teacher lives prompts the question: Will a specifically indigenous culture which is neither Maori nor European but a mingling
of both grow out of the region? Or will a strictly regional culture grow
to provide valuable friction for other multiracial regional cultures
that emerge from Maori–*pakeha* contact in Auckland city and in
other provincial communities? The future of New Zealand's in-

volvement in the wider Pacific world probably depends upon the particular way in which such social contact produces future growth within New Zealand society and helps to modify the national character.

FIVE

MAORITANGA,

THE WAY OF THE MAORIS

Understanding the Maori mind can be just as fruitless as refusal to understand: ask ourselves, none of us would feel easy if we were being observed and questioned by someone humourlessly determined to understand us. There are dangers in the Pakeha writer, with his different traditions, trying to see a Maori from the Maori point of view. He is apt to create a puppet figure of his own, covering his own frustrated aspirations in a brown skin, like a hermit crab.

This sober warning, from W. H. Pearson's "Attitudes to the Maori in some Pakeha Fiction" printed in the *Journal of the Polynesian Society* (September 1958) should be heeded. But for the sensitive and responsible *pakeha* New Zealander, the real desire to understand the Maori will probably come from asking himself, "What is there in Maori culture that is of value to me as a New Zealander?" As the legacy of English cultural tradition becomes transmuted more into a collateral rather than a derivative local tradition, this question becomes more urgent. The Maori had adapted himself to his physical environment long before the European came. He then adapted himself (not entirely successfully, perhaps) to the revolutionary new culture that invaded his islands in the nineteenth century. On the other hand, *pakeha* New Zealanders have unconsciously

87

learned a great deal from Maori ways of life during the past century and a half, and it is time they began to be conscious of the fruitful ways in which they can learn more. Certain aspects of Maori life have survived all the violent dislocations caused by an aggressive, determined, and impetuous invader from a different culture. One suspects that they have survived because they are needed. If they are needed by the Maori, may not some of those aspects of Maori life be needed by the pale-skinned *pakeha*?

Although it is common to hear New Zealanders talk about Maori and *pakeha* ways of life as if they were separate kinds of living, the Maori is more *pakeha*, and the *pakeha* more Maori, than he recognizes. This, at least, is the opinion of E. R. Braithwaite, a recent visitor to New Zealand, whose experiences when published will add yet another "verdict on New Zealand." It might at first seem worthwhile to assess the characteristics of the Maori character by surveying the most outstanding of such overseas visitors' comments, but the exercise would not be really revealing because the intelligent visitor seldom has a satisfactory cultural norm against which to judge the Maoris. Comparisons with native races in other countries colonized by the British have produced accounts that are full of praise for the Maori, but are usually also full of unconscious patronizing. Mark Twain in 1895 provides an example:

The native race is not decreasing but actually increasing slightly. It is another evidence that they are a superior breed of savages. I do not call to mind any savage race that built such good houses, or such strong and ingenious and scientific fortresses, or gave so much attention to agriculture, or had military arts and devices which so nearly approached the white man's. These, taken together with their high abilities in boat building, their tastes and capacities in the ornamental arts, modify their savagery to a semi-civilisation—or at least to a quarter civilisation.

Mr. Braithwaite, on the other hand, is an exception in that he does not patronize; he is an intelligent observer, a novelist and educationalist, who has the great advantage of having been born a Negro in British Guiana and of having lived and traveled in many so-called civilized parts of the world. It is perhaps a disadvantage, however, that he is such a kind and sympathetic analyst of human behavior, for he tends to stress the good qualities and ignore the bad. Nevertheless, he was not exaggerating when he told a London audience that the warmth of the Maoris is unforgettable, and that to leave them was "a tearing apart." *

Braithwaite characterizes the Maoris he met as patient, considerate of others, strong (both spiritually and physically), sensitive, handsome, and fun-loving. He found something of their warmth in the *pakeha* New Zealanders as well, a warmth which he had previously met with only in Africa. On the subject of a color bar, he affirms that he was never conscious in New Zealand of an adverse attitude to himself, but that he did feel that things were not always as happy as they should be between Maori and *pakeha*. He cites examples of discriminatory practices against Maoris (especially over accommodation in the cities) but records a *pakeha* assurance that it is not color discrimination that is responsible. He also points out that New Zealand is the first country with two predominant races—one brown, one white—where he found ready acknowledgment of intermixture. *Pakeha* New Zealanders speak with pride of Maori in-laws; never in the United States or Britain would one hear people speak with pride of a colored son-in-law. In fact, Braithwaite believes that there is no interracial friction in New Zealand. His only adverse comment on the Maori people was the shabby appearance of Maoris in the tourist area of Rotorua, the very area in which most visitors form their opinions of the Maori.

All these comments would seem rather superficial to the man who has written the most penetrating study of race relations in New Zealand, the American psychologist David Ausubel in his book *The Fern and the Tiki* (Sydney, 1960). Nevertheless, they probably represent a slightly more balanced view of the high degree of good will existing in New Zealand than Ausubel is willing to concede. One has the impression that in *The Fern and the Tiki* the author's valiant attempt to attack a sacred cow has led him to exaggerate blindness of devotion to that beast. It is certainly paradoxical that New Zealanders should so vehemently assert that there is no color bar or racial preju-

---

* I can vouch for the accuracy of his statement, for I happened to be a guest on the *marae* where Mr. Braithwaite first lived among the Maori people, and I shared his feeling to the full.

dice in New Zealand despite blatant evidence of prejudiced attitudes to the Maori which Ausubel so neatly categorizes. This paradox must be exposed again and again if race relations are to improve, but the vehemence of New Zealanders' assertions that in New Zealand all is well in comparison with other countries is not wholly to be condemned. For it shows that, whatever his motive, the *pakeha* would like to have a successful multiracial society as one of his country's contributions to a better world.

As a point of departure, I take for granted that an immense fund of good will exists and will continue to exist between *pakeha* and Maori. It may be useful, however, to look at the major cause of unsatisfactory relations in certain areas—ignorance and misunderstanding by *pakehas* of the cultural values and assumptions of the Maori, and Maori shyness or diffidence as well as misunderstanding or distrust in his dealings with *pakehas*. That Maoris show a greater understanding of *pakeha* cultural values and assumptions is a natural consequence of having to live in both a *pakeha* and a Maori world; only a tiny minority of *pakehas* in the normal course of their lives have to adapt to Maori ways of living. This is because Maoris form a cultural as well as a racial minority in New Zealand and in certain ways exercise their right of segregation in order to retain their cultural identity. Among *pakehas* there is a growing awareness, however, of the important differences between a self-imposed segregation (which, because of Maori good will, is never really exclusive) and an enforced segregation of the kind that seemed to be developing when certain iniquitous practices were exposed in a market garden area south of Auckland. Without constant vigilance, such discriminatory practices threaten to develop in the cities as more and more Maoris migrate there. Also, there is a growing awareness among *pakehas* that more knowledge of how Maoris live is to be desired not for the welfare of the Maori alone but for the enrichment of the life of the *pakeha* himself. Education, it is commonly thought by both Maori and *pakeha*, is the key to mutual understanding.

Certain developments within recent years have given cause for hope that a harmonious future is in store for both races. The educational efforts of the universities have begun to leaven the efforts of government officials and organizations and to offer much-needed cultural mediation. As one *pakeha* who lives in both Maori and *pakeha* worlds succinctly phrased it, "You can't work *for* the Maori people, you can only work *with* them." This is, for instance, what adult education and the Department of Anthropology in the University of Auckland are doing.

Maori Adult Education Work

Before 1949, adult education work had been largely confined to *pakehas*, but in that year a remarkable Maori, Maharaia Winiata, became the first Maori to be appointed as an adult education tutor in the Auckland district. The persistence with which he had overcome difficulties in acquiring a higher education was both a cause and a result of his conviction that higher education was one of the major solutions to many of the problems that faced his own people. He became an eloquent advocate of education at all levels, and he worked hard at every gathering of Maori people to convince others of his own suggested solutions of the problems of the day. When he was appointed an adult education tutor in 1949, he had already had much experience of using *hui* (large gatherings) and *tangi* (funeral gatherings) as a medium for such work.

Also in 1949 was established the first chair of anthropology in New Zealand, at Auckland University College. The influence of the Anthropology Department on adult education and upon the education of Maori and *pakeha* alike has been steadily growing, especially as one of the first developments was to appoint a junior lecturer (now an associate professor) in Maori language. Maharaia Winiata came under the influence of the new field of study and in 1952 took up a Nuffield Foundation scholarship to do postgraduate work in social anthropology at the University of Edinburgh. With his thesis, "The Changing Role of the Leader in Maori Society," he became the first Maori to hold a Ph.D. By the time he returned to New Zealand, a second Maori tutor, Matiu te Hau, had been appointed to cover the North Auckland district. In Wellington, too, a Maori tutor had been appointed for the university district in the southern part of the North Island.

The first ten years of attempts to extend adult education to the Maori people was largely experimental. The normal pattern of tutorial classes—a weekly lecture and discussion by a specialist tutor—was not successful because of the difficulties of forming voluntary local organizations that would crystallize local needs. But by working through traditional Maori gatherings, tutors were able to lay the groundwork. Some worthwhile work was also done in promoting traditional arts and crafts. A major step was taken in 1959 when a national conference of young Maori leaders was held at Auckland University. In May 1939, such a conference had been organized by adult education people with the help of Sir Apirana Ngata; though it was a distinct success, it had not been followed up because of the war that took so many young Maoris to the other side of the world. The 1959 national conference was such a success and was felt to have such value that regional conferences were requested, to lead ultimately to another national conference in five or six years' time. About a dozen such regional conferences have already been held, including one to which both *pakeha* and Maori delegates were invited.

The organization of such a conference is a characteristic blend of European and Polynesian traditions. Elders and young men and women who have shown capacity for leadership are invited to attend. They are divided into round tables under an elected chairman to discuss an agenda and papers prepared by specialists. Both the delegates and the topics to be discussed are chosen on the recommendation of local leaders who are organized as a host committee and who work through traditional social and cultural institutions. The aim of the conferences is to make those attending more aware of and critical of the political, economic, educational, and social problems of the Maori people, to foster self-expression and understanding among the young people who may be the leaders of the future, and to provide all those attending with material to be discussed at *hui* and other gatherings of the Maori people. Experience in organizing and conducting such large gatherings and in disseminating knowledge of what educational services are available is also of great value to both Maori and *pakeha* participants.

One of the greatest of modern Maori leaders, Sir Apirana Ngata, advises:

E Tipu, E Rea, mo nga ra o to ao
Ko to ringa ki nga rakau a te pakeha
Hei ora mo to tinana
Ko to ngakau ki nga taonga a o tipuna
Hei tikitiki mo to matenga
Ko to wairua ki Te Atua
Nana nei nga mea katoa

Grow up, Oh tender plant in the mould of your day and age,
With your hands grasping the arts of the pakeha for your
   worldly support,
Your thoughts ever mindful of the treasures of your ancestors
   resting like a proud diadem upon your brow
And your soul dedicated to God, Creator of All Things.

It is a pity that a *pakeha* leader has not produced such an eloquent
piece of advice that would impress itself on the consciousness of the
cultural majority. Instead, the future of race harmony is influenced
by such vague and easily misunderstood terms as "assimilation," "in-
tegration," "segregation," and "symbiosis."

The Culture of the Maori

Among Maoris, one often hears extraordinarily poetic or vigorous
descriptions of the future of the two races. A mundane example of
a description of the present situation was recently offered in im-
promptu fashion by a *kuia* (translate "old woman," but without the
harsh connotations of "old"). She evoked the image of a two-hulled
canoe sailing along the Waitemata (Auckland harbor) with *pakehas*
on one hull and Maoris on the other. The Maoris depend on the
pakehas to shout "rocks ahead" as the canoe negotiates the channels
at the entrance to the harbor, but once in the open sea both the
Maori and the *pakeha* will share one hull. This natural skill with figurative language is seldom found in *pakeha* public speakers. One is
struck by the inability of *pakehas* to express their feelings on this subject and others of emotional implication without falling into pain-
fully embarrassed formality or insensate clichés. This indicates how
much the ancestral treasure of the Maori, *whaikorero*—the art of
speechmaking—is needed by the *pakeha*. Fortunately for the insecure

pakeha who does not have the buttressing warmth of an indigenous culture, the Maori is increasingly showing his willingness to share such treasures with any New Zealander who really appreciates it.

For instance, a recent gathering of Maoris in Auckland showed mixed regret, delight, and admiration when a predominantly *pakeha* group performed a series of Maori action songs and *hakas* (men's war action chants). The performers' seriousness of purpose (but proper gaiety and enthusiasm of manner) bridged a potentially embarrassing cultural gap. Then too, tribal committees are known to elect to positions of responsibility men who have no Maori ancestry but who speak the language and feel, think, and act like Maoris. This is especially true where the balance of power between different tribal groups is felt to be a real problem. An understanding *pakeha* is then of great value to a Maori community. To a certain extent, in fact, *Maoritanga* is not a matter of inheritance; it is a matter of *he manawa*, of "how one feels." Indeed, it is very difficult in New Zealand to say who is a Maori and who is not, for there is no clear division on racial or cultural grounds between *pakeha* and Maori. Thus, the questions "What is Maoritanga?" and "Who is a Maori?" are very difficult to answer.

The word "Maori" in its modern sense of "an indigenous Polynesian inhabitant of New Zealand" apparently developed in the mid-1830s, not in Polynesian usage but in popular and colloquial English usage. It was originally borrowed from the phrase "tangata maori," the noun "tangata" meaning "man," and the adjective "maori" meaning "ordinary," "common," "usual," "normal," "native," or "indigenous." Thus, a *tangata maori* from the Polynesian point of view was someone who had a familiar appearance; strangers, specifically Europeans, with their unfamiliar appearance were naturally excluded by the phrase. The English noun "Maori" very quickly replaced "New Zealander," "native," and other terms denoting the indigenous people of New Zealand. And very quickly too, the English noun was borrowed into the Maori language. Maoris themselves identify strangers among their own race according to their tribal affiliations, but it is interesting to see that in the present decade of increased mobility a new distinction is growing between *tangata whenua* or *tangata marae* (the people who own, or whose ancestors owned, a particular land area or *marae*) and the *rawaho* (immigrant from another tribe or different land area). The *rawaho* can be anyone who claims even the slightest trace of Maori ancestry and who feels that he is a Maori.

The original Maori meaning of the adjective "maori" includes a secondary sense of "clear, intelligible." This explains why "maoritanga" is defined in even the most up-to-date edition of A *Dictionary of the Maori Language* as the abstract noun "explanation, meaning." But when Sir James Carroll and other leaders of the Young Maori Party wanted a term to denote the way of life of their people, they took the completely-assimilated modern meaning of the word "Maori" —which, thanks to the *pakeha*, transcended tribal boundaries—and coined a new meaning for "Maoritanga." The meaning of the term is debated and discussed, analyzed and defined, used and abused with great frequency in the present upsurge of interest in Maori culture and traditional ways of thinking, feeling, and acting. A second Maori renaissance seems to be under way, aided by this all-embracing term and strengthened by the success of the first one in the early decades of this century.

But who is a Maori? For census and other official purposes, a Maori is defined as a person of at least half Maori blood—an increasingly difficult criterion to apply, and one with racist overtones. Within the census definition, New Zealand had a population of 137,151 Maoris in 1956, 88,440 of whom (over 63 per cent) were said to be full Maoris. An additional 25,307 people with some Maori ancestry were recorded. This is possibly a conservative figure, but it reduces the percentage of full Maoris among those claiming Maori ancestry to about 54 per cent. It indicates just how much intermarriage there has been between the Maori and later immigrant peoples. Changes in the pattern of intermarriage can be detected, but no significant decline or increase in the rate is taking place. Few Maoris are ashamed of non-Maori blood, nor is the phenomenon of "passing for white" so common in other countries widely known in New Zealand. Most *pakehas* are proud of whatever Maori ancestry they have. When one hears a New Zealander say, "He's got a bit of Maori blood in him," it seldom implies hostility, even if it does reveal unconscious assumptions about race superiority or inferiority. Although there is no "in-between" world inhabited by half-castes, most half-castes are usually thought of as half-caste Maoris, probably because of unconscious racial prejudice among ignorant *pakehas* but mainly because Maori communities offer them a greater sense of belonging. The warmth of Maoritanga as compared with the uneasy society of the *pakeha* is thus illustrated.

When the cream of New Zealand culture—the rugby football team —goes onto the field to play a game, it begins with a *haka*. This overt adoption of a Maori tradition by *pakehas* is taken so much for granted that it causes no comment. When a predominantly *pakeha* team turns to one of its members whom they recognize as a Maori (mainly on the basis of his skin color) to lead the *haka*, they show natural tact and sense of respect as well as need. When that Maori does not know enough about his own culture to teach his team this dance of defiance but has to ask one of his kinsmen privately to help him live up to what is expected of him, we have a fine image of the present-day cultural predicament of New Zealanders. The need, both Maori and *pakeha*, is there.

By continuing an essentially rural life in a modified form of the traditional *pa*, many tribes in the nineteenth century managed to preserve enough of their traditional ways of living to transmit arts and crafts, social habits, spiritual values, and traditional culture. By retiring behind the *aukati* (boundary of European settlement) after "the white man's anger" (the civil wars of the nineteenth century), the dispossessed King Movement tribes and their King Country hosts were able to preserve even more of their traditional culture. Taranaki attempts to rejuvenate Maori ways of life by using a blend of European and Maori culture were rendered futile by *pakeha* opposition to Te Whiti but were vindicated by later efforts of the Young Maori Party. Much of the work done in the nineteenth century and early twentieth century to preserve Maori culture was overshadowed by Maori success in grasping the material arts of the *pakeha*, especially in the field of health and education. But New Zealanders are only now beginning to feel the benefits of that preservation.

Ever since the renaissance of the early years of the twentieth century, and because *pakeha* society has tacitly consented to the Maori's right to withdraw or mingle at need, a good pattern of race relations has grown up, so that a Maori who lives like a *pakeha* will be accepted as a *pakeha*, and at the same time, a part-Maori can still be accepted as a full member of the Maori community. Under these conditions, traditional Maori culture has been both preserved and modified. It is now being disseminated through educational channels that are a blend of Maori and *pakeha* tradition.

The core of Maoritanga according to Sir Apirana Ngata, was the language. New Zealand schools, until the 1930s (and even later in some areas), did their best to prevent Maoris from speaking their ancestral language. The barbaric theory upon which the policy of punishing children for not speaking English was based was that speaking Maori would hinder the acquisition of the language of the real world in which the children would have to live when they grew up. Academic studies in bilingualism are producing a revolutionary change in educationalists' attitudes, and the teaching of Maori and in Maori is an increasingly desired objective in the schools. The greatest bar to progress now is the lack of suitably qualified teachers. Although much prejudice has to be overcome, intensification of Maori studies in the universities is beginning to have its effects in the teachers' colleges. When two-year courses for training teachers are extended to the more desirable three or four years, as in other countries, there may be more room in the syllabus for an expansion of Maori studies, which are as yet rudimentary and optional.

The *marae* and the community activities associated with it are of central importance to Maoritanga. *Whaikorero*, the speechmaking on the *marae*, is the finest flower of the Maori language, including as it does the *tauparapara* (opening chant or incantation), *mihi* (formal greetings), *poroporoaki* (valedictory greetings to the dead), the speech itself, and the closing *waiata* (song). At least, this is how a Ngati-porou *kaumatua* (elder) has defined a true speech. Maoritanga includes many different tribal customs and many forms of speechmaking. The more formal parts of the speech tend to be whittled away by time; for instance, the speaker who made the five-part rhetorical analysis above deplored the modern practice of dropping the *waiata*. What is so foreign and even distasteful to some *pakeha* thinking is the way in which Maori orators prefer the indirect figurative speech of the formal *whaikorero* to the direct, sometimes logical, and usually reasonable argumentation in the discourse of *pakeha* culture.

But metaphors, similes, and allusions to the oral classics of the Maori people are not merely attempts to show off one's learning; they establish the understanding, the wisdom, and the sensibility of the speaker at the same time as they persuade. And the principal method of persuasion is to bring a present proposal into fruitful harmony with traditional values with an economy of effort inherent only in poetry. The *pakeha* could learn much from the Maori about the usefulness and value of poetry, even in his own language.

Victorian emasculation of Maori myths, the "prettying up" of Maori legends to provide children with quaint stories, the delay in publishing and disseminating the oral material, and the slowness of the *pakeha* to develop a feeling of intimate relationship with the land are possibly the main reasons for the failure to develop a true cross-fertilization of Maori and *pakeha* culture until now. Allen Curnow and Roger Oppenheim, in *The Penguin Book of New Zealand Verse* (edited by Allen Curnow; Harmondsworth, 1960), have made a brave attempt to bridge the gap by translating six poems into meaningful English. But probably the most heartening sign of the closing of the gap is the poetry (in English) of Hone Tuwhare. Only when a *pakeha* hears Tuwhare reading his poems to a Maori audience does he understand how much he has missed of their meaning and appeal in cold print. For behind the customary English words there runs a sensitivity to rhythms and images, a sensibility both strange and familiar, which is often struggling with alien rhythms and idioms but frequently and triumphantly conquering them. His poems are a modest beginning, but an important beginning, of a new dimension in New Zealand literature.

The conduct of a *hui* could teach the *pakeha* many lessons of great benefit to him. For instance, much of the prejudiced sectarianism of Europe that has unconsciously been transplanted to New Zealand is attenuated and even extinguished in Maori society because of the overriding spirit of hospitality, kinship obligation, and friendliness. It is unthinkable that anyone should be excluded from a gathering because of his religious beliefs or that sectarianism should prevent the free exchange of ideas on a *marae*. Pakehas could also learn the art of talking things out until unanimity is reached.

The conduct of a *hui* is also valuable for demonstrating that a modern modification of a fundamentally aristocratic culture may facilitate true social ease and personal security in a way that a brash egalitarianism may not. The ease of social contact in a gathering of such huge numbers as is frequent at a large *hui* is partly a result of communal living, for visitors sleep communally in the meeting house (*whare hui*) and dine communally in another large hall (*whare kai*). It is also partly due to Maoris' deeply felt respect for the basic rights and privileges of both host and guest. The *tangata whenua* are kings on their own *marae* and are accorded their rightful respect. But the kings make themselves slaves to their guests without loss of dignity or sense of patronage. Democratic feelings are strong, but they do not kill respect for leaders, whether traditional or modern. And those leaders use their *mana* (prestige) to make everyone feel they belong. The stranger very soon discovers how a "Maori heart" working within a living adaptation of an ancient aristocratic culture can develop a rich, meaningful society. When one observes the simple dignity and unconscious but respectful assurance with which most young Maoris both defer to and resist their elders, or, for example, approach the throne room of King Koroki, one cannot help comparing them favorably with their *pakeha* counterparts whose natural respect is often overlaid with a shallow cynicism and scarcely veiled hostility, which their society has taught them is an acceptable way of confronting authority.

Leadership in traditional Maori society was vested in a fourfold hierarchy of *ariki* (whose birth gave him the highest *mana*), *rangatira* (chiefs of aristocratic lineage), *kaumatua* and *kuia* (male and female elders), and *tohunga* (wise man, keeper of esoteric lore, navigator, and healer). The *kaumatua* is the most commonly found survivor of this society, but in some areas descendants of the original aristocratic class exist beside specifically modern leaders who have arisen in accordance with modern needs for specialists. The *tohunga* still survives, but he has been shorn of some of the functions that made him a dangerous substitute for *pakeha* medical science. The Tohunga Suppression Act of 1908 is largely responsible for this, and by repealing it in 1963 Parliament acknowledged that the modern *tohunga* can and does fill a special need in the field of spiritual or psychiatric healing. The traditional leaders thus still perform an important function in modern Maori society, but there can be no doubt that the modern leader, grown out of an increasing complexity in New Zealand's multiracial society, is of ever greater importance. But his *mana* is intimately connected with his ability to share that leadership with his chiefs and elders.

Elected *rangatahi* organize youth clubs, sports clubs, dance bands, and other entertainment and educational groups, and specialists without traditional *mana* also serve on *komiti marae*. Linguistic borrowings from English (*komiti*: committee; *tiamana*: chairman; *hekeretari*: secretary) indicate how much *pakeha* influence has penetrated *marae* organizations. Tribal committees, initiated in 1945, are the basis for intertribal cooperation and have, with democratic evolution, become the only organization (apart from Maori Women's Welfare Leagues) to reach a national level. The efficient working of this new structure depends largely on cooperation between modern and traditional leaders. Other national, social, and political movements which aim at uniting the Maori people and at giving Maoritanga a voice (such as the Ratana and King Movements, Kauhanganui, and Kotahitanga) have thrown up leaders who are more traditional than modern, even though most are elective. The four Maori members of Parliament belong to the Labour Party and to the Ratana Movement, and many Maoris feel that they do not speak for the whole Maori people. Perhaps the modern leaders who command the most universal respect, however, are religious leaders, for an important element of Maoritanga is a profound religious sense. This is a result of the blending of attitudes of traditional Maori society with the beliefs brought by the early European missionaries. The respect accorded to missionaries (despite their frequently bitter sectarianism) is still a strong tradition and blends well with respect for one's ancestors and one's spiritual leaders. Nearly 20,000 Maoris belong to the church of the Maori cult of Ratana (.9 per cent of the population of New Zealand, 15 per cent of the Maori population), and about a quarter as many profess to be Ringatu, also a Maori cult. A number of other specifically Maori adaptations of Christian beliefs exist, but most Maoris belong to the Church of England, the Roman Catholic Church, and the Methodist Church. The Church of Latter Day Saints also has a large following in certain areas, and in other areas the Presbyterian Church is gaining ground. But whatever the particular version of Christian worship, feelings of reverence are deeply rooted in pre-Christian attitudes that reinforce and enrich present-day worship. *Karakia* (prayers) play a natural part in all gatherings, secular, or religious, and traditional feelings about *mana* subordinate any sectarian feelings about who should conduct such prayers in a mixed gathering.

It is very important for *pakehas* to understand the strength of religious feeling among Maoris, for it permeates all aspects of living in a way that it does not in secularized *pakeha* society. For instance, it goes a long way to explain why Maoris feel strongly their need to withdraw from *pakeha* society and why they are in some cases reluctant to share the treasures of their ancestors with the *pakeha*. Perhaps the most eloquent way to demonstrate this is to quote from Sir Apirana Ngata's *The Price of Citizenship* (Wellington, 1943) his translation of a letter from a guardian of the *whakapapa* (table of genealogy) of the Whanau-a-Apanui people. Ngata had asked for genealogical tables to show the maternal descent of Lieutenant Te Moana Ngarimu, the Ngati-porou soldier who earned the Victoria Cross in 1943 for valor in Tunisia.

To Weihana,
Here are these heirlooms, which are sent to you to be forwarded. Great is my sorrow at the delay, but I have been unable to avoid it. It is not that I have objected to complying with the request, but it is that I have experienced a strange feeling, when my mind was addressing itself to the task required of me. My mind was lost and a weakness affected my body, and I knew that this was on account of the passing of these treasures to a strange place for strange hands to fondle. At such moments I was constrained to fast and to pray in my church, that I might be given strength, and granted the grace to carry out this work for the sake of the great day approaching of the Nation's celebration. You will see my writing in the acompanying tables, the trembling of the hand, the reluctance of the pen to transcribe, even when forming such a familiar name as Pita's. Note how shakily the lines from Te Aomoengariki are traced down. It was only the other day to yesterday, that I became my former self and decided to make a new copy of all the tables, namely of those I now send you.
My own feeling, O Wei, in this matter is, that we should exercise all humility for the honour bestowed by God on our young relative.

Although I have so constructed the genealogical tables as to converge on him only, that is as it should be, for he is the occasion for the sentiment, which convulses the country. They are for the eyes of those who understand; for there are men who have eyes with which to see, but do not see. This youth, Moana, was like an axe in the hands of one, who felled a tree. Who should have the honour? The axe, or the man? Was he not indeed an axe in the hands of his Maker? It is true that the axe should have honour, a little honour, but the glory belongs to our Father in heaven. That should not be dimmed by the fame of the axe. Regards, from just me,

T. Tawhai

Ngata's comment on the letter is as follows:

So, my dear friend Timutimu, I put you on record in the best possible setting for the sentiments, which have been drawn from your innermost being, which some few understand and all must respect and admire. The time is long past, when the heirlooms and the treasures of Maori culture can be hidden in the memories of a fond few or in laboriously compiled manuscripts dedicated to descendants, who may never prize them. They can be forgotten, my friend, and lost. And they should not be lost. So you and I and others should have them kept, as the Pakeha keeps his records and knowledge, in print on bookshelves, that those who care may read and learn.

A. T. Ngata

"The great day approaching of the Nation's celebration" was the Ngarimu *hui* at Ruatoria. No Maori gathering has ever been put on record so completely. A souvenir program contained *peruperu* (action songs), *haka*, and *waiata*. The Polynesian Society published a booklet called *The Ngarimu Hui* with superb photographs by John Pascoe, and the Government Film Unit and cameramen of the United States Marine Corps recorded the official Victoria Cross investiture and other features of the *hui* on sound film. But probably of greatest cultural significance is Ngata's book *The Price of Citizenship*, for it exhibits with vivid brevity the way Maoritanga is going to survive. The citation approving the posthumous award of the Victoria Cross to Ngarimu is for any reader an eloquent and masterly piece of writing, a part of New Zealand's own cultural tradition. But it is more than that, for by the indirect allusion so prized by Maori orators it places

Ngarimu's Tunisian deeds in clear relation to the battle of Te Mani-aroa which took place on the East Coast in the seventeenth century. There, on a rocky slope a few miles north of Te Araroa, the Whanau-a-Apanui ancestors of Ngarimu conquered in circumstances similar to those of 1943 the Ngati-porou ancestors of Ngarimu. Maori deeds in a *pakeha* world are thus seen as part of a deep tradition.

The linking of a changing present to a receding past is nowhere more significantly achieved than at the most important of all *hui*, the *tangi*. Something of the importance to a Maori of *tangihanga* (funerals) can be gathered from Sir Peter Buck's account of death and burial in his *Coming of the Maori* (Wellington, 1949). And something of the therapeutic effect of traditional wailing and emotion is also analyzed. *Pakehas* do not understand this, for their culture emphasizes the value of a "stiff upper lip" attitude to funerals. British feeling that it doesn't do to let one's feelings go on such occasions leads to a belief that formality and "not intruding" on other people's grief is the best way to deal with mourning. Maoris, however, prefer to take their dead to a *marae* (preferably an ancestral one) to lie in state, while friends and relatives come in large numbers to pay their respects and alleviate the family suffering. The *tangata whenua* feel morally obliged to provide food and sleeping facilities for the mourn-ers; the mourners feel morally obliged to remain till at least a day after interment to cheer up the bereaved.

Pakehas in the nineteenth century condemned the *tangi* because of the risk of spreading infectious disease, especially because the corpse was sometimes kept above ground for over a week to allow distant relatives to pay their respects. Sir Peter Buck and other Maori leaders managed to forestall an attempt to abolish the *tangi* by law and instead helped to enforce sanitation laws and fix a limit of three days in summer and four in winter for the lying in state. *Pakeha* em-ployers in the twentieth century deplore the sudden absences of Maori employees for four days, especially because some Maoris do not ask permission to be absent because they assume that *pakehas* will not understand their needs and obligations. Perhaps nothing better illus-trates the way in which Maoris try to "grow up in the mold of their day and age" than their attempt to modify one of their most deeply rooted customs in order to suit an unfeeling *pakeha* demand like this.

For *tangihanga* customs are being subtly modified without losing the spirit of the customs. For instance, an elder of the Ngati-maniapoto tribe has described the way in which the automobile is making it possible for mourners to pay their respects in the early morning and again after working hours without violating their obligations to *pakeha* society. He also described the custom of leaving silver coins (*moni roimata*, "the tears of the mourners") to help the bereaved family and the *komiti marae* to pay for the *tangi*; characteristically, the money is laid out in front of the meeting house, and its symbolic functions are stressed by formal dedication. In the evenings, the mourners will stay up all night if necessary to comfort the afflicted and to indulge in traditional expressions of grief.

The greatest pressure on the Maori to modify his customs is felt in the city. The traditional wailing of the women on a rural *marae* affects only those attending a *tangi*, but in a city, where Maoris live cheek-by-jowl with *pakehas*, where there are few traditional *maraes*, and where the business of making a living impinges heavily on social, religious, and moral obligations, many features of a traditional *tangi* may disturb non-participants. Nevertheless, as an East Coast speaker has explained, when someone in the city dies, the *tupapaku* will lie in state in a suburban home, a *hangi* will be made in the backyard, Maori tears will be wept, and Maori speeches will be made even if the *kaumatua* has to give the *mihi* from another room. A new kind of Maoritanga is growing in the cities, a Maoritanga with strong ties in the rural areas where a Maori knows his *turangawaewae* ("footstool" —the standing place for the feet of any Maori) to be.

One of the Maori's most basic treasures is his self-identification in terms of *whanaungatanga* (kinship) and his feeling of attachment to the land of his ancestors. Relatively few *pakehas* experience this feeling, but it will undoubtedly become a more powerful feeling in the future. One would think that more and more Maoris are going to lose this feeling in the cities as they become "detribalized," but, at present, it is in fact one of the strong bonds that help a Maori to live in the city with a minimum of difficulty. The lively traditions of *waiata*, action songs, *poi*, *haka*, and other dances and songs and of arts and crafts is also being fostered in the cities by adult education, Maori clubs, and other cultural associations. The landless Maori will probably be the most common type of Maori in the future, but he will be the one who brings the values of Maoritanga to the education of the *pakeha.*

Pakeha tolerance of Maori cultural differences may seem to contradict the generalization often made about New Zealanders that they are intolerant of those who do not conform to their narrowly material concept of proper behavior. But when one looks more closely, it will be found that a great deal of the tolerance is in fact indifference. Because so few *pakehas* are intimately acquainted with life in a *pa,* they tend to judge Maori behavior as it is exhibited within their own culture. And the Maori is an adept at adapting his behavior to accepted standards by drawing upon his enormous sense of fun and friendliness. "Pulling the leg" of the *pakeha* and self-effacing jokes are superb means of providing social lubrication. Telling the *pakeha* what he wants to know rather than causing social friction with an unpalatable truth is typical. *Pakehas* find Maoris excellent companions to work with because of their easy social manner, because of the uncanny ease and grace with which they handle machinery, and because of their immense good will toward those who do not get as much fun out of life as they do. With such advantages, future relations between the two races should not deteriorate if the *pakeha* learns through knowledge rather than indifference.

This chapter has suggested some areas of Maori experience and culture that might beneficially modify national culture. Not less important than the possibility of living a fuller and richer life is the possibility that, by understanding a distinctive culture within their own borders, New Zealanders may better equip themselves for involvement in affairs of the Pacific and Southeast Asia. By appointing a Maori as New Zealand's representative in Malaya, the authorities have shown what an important role Maoris themselves can and will play in the country's future international relations.

It is unnecessary here to outline what the Maori might learn from the *pakeha,* for there is a vast body of advice on the subject, and *pakeha* humanitarianism is embodied in welfare legislation and in everyday contacts with Maoris. It is saddeningly true, however, that many Maoris fall short in attaining standards of health and material comfort equal to that of most *pakehas,* and that even greater efforts will have to be made to solve such "social problems," as they are delicately called. Maoritanga proclaims the intention to achieve such a limited aim, but only as part of the fourfold aim expressed by Sir Apirana Ngata: to adapt to new circumstances, to make use of the material advantages of western civilization, to retain whatever is of value in the treasures of one's ancestors, and to conduct the effort to put spiritual values before the material with proper acknowledgment to God. A harmonious blend of all four aims is the true spirit of Maoritanga.

Maori and *pakeha* alike must learn (and they seem to be learning) an even greater appreciation of their cultural heritage, both Polynesian and European, if they are to develop and maintain in health all their faculties. An indigenous multiracial culture in which matters of the intellect and of the spirit are prized as much as matters of bodily health and comfort may yet arise from the educational friction supplied by more intimate contact between the two most important cultures at present flourishing in New Zealand.

SIX

From Bonanza

to Export Drive

There can be no doubt that the peculiar form of isolationism that prevails in New Zealand is produced by the occupational habits of her farmers. Preoccupation with producing wool, butter, cheese, and meat for a seemingly inexhaustible market created by a continuation of Great Britain's nineteenth-century concentration upon industrialization has tended to make New Zealanders think that all one needs to worry about is producing the goods and they will sell themselves. This attitude was probably engendered in the pioneers very early by bonanza conditions. No one needed to worry about a market for gold; all one had to do was find it and mine it. No one needed to worry about a market for wool; all one had to worry about was the price offering. An open, undeveloped countryside made it fairly easy to adapt to any changes in prices. When prices for pastoral products seemed more favorable than grain prices, for instance, the Canterbury lowland farmer changed his habits to suit the market. The consequence of having one's main market on the other side of the world induced the feeling that one could not really manipulate that market. The New Zealander soon learned to keep his eyes on his own garden.

Nevertheless, the situation changed fundamentally as soon as a great deal of money had been invested in fixed assets such as improved pasture, mechanical and electrical equipment, and highly efficient processing factories, and as soon as most of the potentially productive land had been broken in and subdivided into fairly inflexible "economic units." Vested interest demanded ever more urgently that the market be manipulated to suit the farmer, and as soon as bulk purchasing by the United Kingdom government ceased in 1954, attention had to be diverted from actual production to problems of expanding the market. It can be confidently predicted that more attention will be paid to market research in the future, and that publicity from such activities will ensure that New Zealanders will take an informed interest in the countries with which they trade. Production for a wholesale and bulk market will increasingly develop into production for a diversity of wholesale and retail markets, so that "trade" will signify for New Zealanders a much more intimate connection with other countries than it does at present.

The Importance of Overseas Trade

New Zealand has always been heavily dependent upon overseas trade for her development and prosperity. Economic fluctuations during the past decade or so have therefore produced an almost neurotic intensification of propaganda to increase and diversify exports. United Nations figures for total external trade per head of population have put the tiny territories of Netherlands Antilles and Singapore at the head of nations heavily engaged in external trade. But these exceptionally active countries are followed by eleven countries whose external trade per head is betwen £200 and £300, with New Zealand about halfway down the list at £246. (New Zealand's trade per head has in fact quadrupled since 1939.) It is worthy of note, then, that in the early sixties of this century New Zealand ranks with the Scandinavian countries, follows not far behind Iceland, Belgium, and Switzerland, stands slightly ahead of Canada and well ahead of the United Kingdom and Australia, and is over three times as heavily engaged in external trade as South Africa or the United States of America. And because imports are dependent to a very great extent upon exports, New Zealanders are very conscious of the importance of their export industries.

Early trade was almost entirely with Australia, but practically nothing is known about the volume of exports and imports before

1853. One can easily guess at the kinds of import needed in the pioneer settlements; timber, potatoes, and wool were established as the major exports by this date. One might generalize, perhaps rashly, by asserting that wool has been the staple export throughout the subsequent history of New Zealand, and that its pre-eminence in bringing in foreign currency has been challenged only under special conditions. The first and most spectacular of such special conditions was the gold bonanza of the 1860s; the second was a much less important but nonetheless significant grain bonanza of the 1870s; the third (a true development of natural resources) was the important diversification of the pastoral industry (meat, butter, and cheese) in the 1880s, prompted largely by the development of refrigeration and speedier sea transport. The gold and grain bonanzas tended to deplete the natural resources of New Zealand but helped to bring capital, equipment, and population. These eventually made possible the wiser exploitation of the true source of New Zealand's wealth—her grasslands and the animals that graze upon them.

There were no animals of any great importance in New Zealand before the European came. The Maoris added rats and dogs to the only other indigenous mammal, the bat. Early explorers attempted to liberate animals in the islands, but pigs and goats seem to have been the only ones to survive. Bay whalers brought "cattle," a category which included almost all the domestic animals found in Australian settlements. Farmers brought more livestock than any of the explorers, missionaries, or bay whalers and sealers. The Wakefield settlements, agricultural by intention, very soon branched out into pastoral farming and other activities. Pigs and goats quickly took to the bush and became the ancestors of the present wild pigs and goats. The existence of large sheep runs in Australia and the discovery of suitable land in New Zealand soon led to the large-scale import of sheep. In little over a century, the human population of New Zealand has grown from about 200,000 to 2½ millions; in the same period, the sheep population has grown from a few hundred to over 50 million.

At the present time, about half of the total area of New Zealand is devoted to the raising of sheep. The pre-eminence of the pastoral industries in the New Zealand economy as a whole may be gauged by the fact that almost a third of all production, both primary and secondary, is pastoral production. By "pastoral," the Census and Statistics Department means grassland farming other than dairying, poultry farming, and beekeeping. This distinction is a little artificial, for New Zealand dairy farms often carry sheep as well, and mixed farming is very common among the owners of small holdings. About half the national production by value comes from farming (i.e., pastoral, dairying, poultry, bees, and agriculture). Farming accounts for over 90 per cent of the Dominion's exports. Wool, meat, butter, and cheese alone have provided between 75 per cent and 90 per cent of total exports every year since 1938. Wool has throughout the period been the most important export. There can be no doubt that New Zealand's prosperity is founded on her grassland farming and that her continuing prosperity is largely dependent upon the orderly development of the productivity of the industries based on her grasslands.

Grassland farming in New Zealand was made possible by ingenious utilization of the natural grasslands in the first instance, and thereafter by constant research and experiments with sown pasture. At the present time, about 32 million of the 44 million acres classified as "occupied land" in New Zealand are grasslands used for pastoral farming. Of these, about 18 million are sown pastures. The rest are principally the tussock lands of the high country of the South Island, the carrying capacity of which has been reduced through overstocking, depredation by rabbits, and possibly also the burning-off techniques used to make them suitable for pasture. Arguments for and against burning as an influence in the declining productivity of the natural grasslands have been raging for half a century. Rabbits have been successfully reduced, but economic pressures seem to be as great as ever to stock tussock lands as densely as possible. Natural tussock is not suitable fodder until winter burning has destroyed spiny Discaria and other weeds and allowed the spring growth of the tussock to provide young and tender feed. The new growth is kept pruned by the sheep themselves and provides some feed to complement the intertussock vegetation.

Wool Production

Early attempts by New Zealand Company colonists to establish sheep runs were prompted by the low prices at which sheep or cattle could be bought in Australia in the late 1830s and early 1840s, by the possibility of running the sheep or cattle on lands that had not yet been opened up for sale, by the small but increasing local market for meat, and (probably pre-eminently) by uncertainty whether large-scale agricultural development was possible. The uncertainty was exacerbated by the slowness with which surveying and selling of suitable agricultural land was taken in hand. The pattern of development and the motives for it are perhaps best expressed in the letters of the Deans family.[1] William Deans and his brother John began pastoral farming at Riccarton, now a suburb of Christchurch. Their immediate market was to be visiting whalers, and their speculative market a colony which they felt sure would be established very soon at Port Cooper, as it was then called.

John Deans went to Australia for livestock, and the two brothers, their friends, and servants, began squatting (with government and Maori permission) upon 33,000 acres, including twenty acres previously plowed and cropped by people from Sydney, who had abandoned them a year or so before. They immediately settled into mixed farming and grazed their sheep and cows between the natural fences formed by the branches of the river they named the Avon. Their letters are full of the details of their experience with crops and animal husbandry and with native plants, fish, and birds. But of greatest interest is their experience with grazing sheep, an occupation at first of less concern to them than to their "neighbor," Greenwood. Soon the rush was on. Squatters from Australia were joined by English and Scottish capitalists eager to buy stock from drought-stricken Australian graziers weighed down by economic depression, and to transfer them to new pastures in the South Island or the Wairarapa.

Sheep acclimatized to the high country of the South Island are of the type of the Merino developed in Australia from South African,

[1] Edited by John Deans as *Pioneers of Canterbury* (1937).

English and Indian strains. A habit peculiar to the breed in New Zealand is to climb to the highest peaks and feed systematically down to the lower levels, whence they are removed to lower pastures before the snows come. On lower, hill country farms, it was early discovered that half-bred sheep were better adapted and more profitable, so the practice was developed of putting a long-wool English ram (Leicester or Lincoln were the most common) to a Merino ewe. This provided some incentive for high country graziers to raise some breeding ewes for farmers in the foothills. Cross-breeding of Merinos with Romney Marsh on more productive low country land was also extensively practiced, and in the North Island at least, the Romney became of great importance. Meanwhile, between 1866 and 1868 on the Corriedale sheep station in North Otago, experiments with inbreeding the half-bred progeny of Romneys and Merinos (and, later, of Leicesters and Merinos) pioneered the development of New Zealand's own special breed. This breed, the Corriedale, was stabilized in the seventies as a wool-bearing animal best adapted to a variety of New Zealand conditions. It has since proved to be the ideal all-purpose sheep, giving place to the Romney only when pastures are greatly improved. New Zealand has for some time exported stud sheep of this local breed to South Africa, South America, North America, and elsewhere. Some 4 to 5 per cent of New Zealand's sheep population are now Corriedale, but upwards of 60 per cent are Romney, about 20 per cent cross-bred, and 8 per cent half-bred. About 2 or 3 per cent are Merino, and another 2 per cent Southdown.

The rapid increase of the Romney Marsh is associated with the more difficult type of sheep farming that was developed in Southland and in the very different environment of the North Island. Unlike the tussock-covered hill country of the South Island or the sparsely forested plains below it, most of the North Island was bush-clad (i.e., forested). The settlers developed the technique of "cut and burn"; undergrowth and young trees were cut during the winter and left to dry out during the early summer, whereupon a fire lit in favorable winds would sweep through the forest, leaving a charred mass of stumps and logs. Grass seed planted in the warm ash would produce sufficient growth in the following spring to support the flock. Cattle were then put in with the sheep to keep as much secondary growth as possible from establishing itself. But gradual decline in fertility and carrying capacity followed, as it had in the tussock country. Before he could plow or carry out other preliminaries to the establishment of even a small area of good permanent pasture, the farmer was faced with the tremendous burden of stumping—clearing the smoke-blackened trunks and deep-rooted stumps from the paddocks (fields). Greater rainfall caused erosion and forced the use of Romneys, Lincolns, or other breeds to make the pioneering of such land profitable.

Wool prices dropped in the late 1860s and early 1870s, but the sheep population and the area of sown pasture steadily increased. On 15 February 1882, the day the first shipment of about 5,000 carcasses of frozen mutton and lamb left Port Chalmers, there were over 13 million sheep in New Zealand (two thirds of them in the South Island), and nearly 4 million acres in sown pasture. Experimental breeding received new impetus, and the short-wool Southdown became important in the breeding of sheep for meat. The Romney also increased in importance, because it produced better meat than other breeds that were as well adapted to the extremes of wetness and heaviness of soil that go with good pasture.

The Meat and Dairy Industries

At about this time, new impetus was given to experimental improvement of pasture, and the fattening farm on low-lying, fertile, well-watered land began to come into its own. "Canterbury lamb" was gradually promoted in the British market during the next dozen years, until frozen mutton became New Zealand's second most important export. By 1963, New Zealand had become the biggest meat-exporting country in the world. But the development of the meat industry was no bonanza development like the gold rushes or the short-lived attempt to convert Canterbury and North Otago into the granary of New Zealand. The refrigeration venture was pioneered by a financial company into whose hands many large sheep stations had fallen because of financial stringency consequent upon falling wool prices. The meat works which developed throughout the country in the 1880s had to be organized efficiently, markets had to be opened up, transport had to be organized and equipped. The expensive but effective state-financed railway construction program of the seventies contributed enormously to the development of the new industry. Rapid progress in the midst of economic depression was a testimonial to New Zealanders' vigor, foresight, hard work, and ability to adapt to new challenges. The meat industry of today owes a great deal to the energies of the men of the 1880s.

The improvement of pastures for meat-producing sheep helped pave the way for the development of yet another major pastoral industry—dairy farming. Dairy farming also developed in response to a political pressure. The Advances to Settlers' Act 1894 was designed to foster closer settlement in a country still sparsely settled and as yet divided into many isolated geographical areas linked only by railways. Closer settlement led to a new political and economic hegemony, too, and leadership in farming communities passed from the South Island "heartland" region to the regions dominated by dairying. The Liberal-Labour government was the political outcome of an alliance between the small farmer and the urban worker; the alliance eventually broke down, and the Reform Party (which took office in 1912 and retained it until 1928) became the political voice of the new hegemony.

Early experience with cattle in New Zealand may also be found in the Deans' letters. Unlike sheep, which were primarily raised for wool and only secondarily for meat, cattle served three purposes of almost equal importance. As beasts of burden, they pulled the drays, plows, and other agricultural implements; to this day they are still treated as farm implements in "bush burn" country, where they crush fern and keep secondary growth in check so that sheep may be run on the burned-off land. Secondly, they provided beef for local consumption and salted beef for settlers and soldiers farther afield. And thirdly, they provided milk, butter, and cheese for local consumption and (in the case of cheese) even for Australian needs.

As the Merino was to the sheepman, so the Shorthorn (mainly the Durham developed in Australia from South African, Indian, and some English strains) was the all-purpose breed to the cattleman. The Shorthorn quickly became acclimatized to both high country and plains. If the cost of each beast had been comparable with the cost of sheep, if returns from investment had been faster, and if the produce to be gained from fattening cattle had been more readily exportable, it is quite possible that large tracts of what is now known as sheep country would have become primarily cattle country. After generations of experience with sheep, New Zealanders would have to learn a great deal to reach the same peak of efficiency with beef cattle. In the early days, the Scots in North Otago were leaders in attempting to win out in competition with sheep. There, although expert husbandry probably contributed, it was climate that gave the Shorthorn economic superiority over the Merino.

The cattle industry was spurred by the gold rushes, which, unfortunately, lasted for only a few years. During this period, there was a great deal of anxious experimenting by small holders attempting to find the right animals for local environments. Dairy animals on ships had previously been goats, but cows were beginning to be used more frequently as steamships took over the long voyages from England. Such animals were sold at the end of the journey. In the sixties, the milk-producing Jerseys and Holstein-Friesians were first imported into New Zealand and quickly increased in number in the North Island. Shorthorns and Ayrshire cattle still predominated in the South Island. In 1963, 85 per cent of dairy cows in New Zealand were Jerseys.

The coming of refrigeration in the eighties, the opening up of the North Island by the "bush burn" technique (which required cattle to crush ferns), the gradual eclipse in the South Island of the "bullocky" and his beast of burden, the need for highly fertile land for dairying —all these ensured that the cattle industry would be largely limited to the North Island. The hegemony of the South Island and of the sheep barons began to give way as the pioneering dairy farmer and intensive mixed farmer developed rich pastureland in the North. The Australian squatter's "Go East, young man" became the Mainlander's "Go North, young man."

Condliffe, the economist, has paid high tribute to the efforts of the pioneering dairy farmers in bringing about the economic transformation of the country after 1890. He places great emphasis upon the development of cooperative dairy factories, the first of which was set up in Taranaki in the late 1860s. These factories proved to be a potent instrument of technical education, producing higher and higher standards. Vigorous factory managers, backed by the most productive farmers supplying cream or milk to the cooperative organization, put pressure on the more slapdash or inefficient farmers to ensure that their factory would compete well with others. A state system of grading butter and cheese (carried out by dairy inspectors appointed by the Department of Agriculture) and state advisory services on rural cooperation were aimed at encouraging profitable small holdings to create closer settlement. In effect, they created at the same time a very efficient system of marketing that channeled back to the farmer over 80 per cent of the wholesale price of butter and over 70 per cent of the wholesale price of cheese on the London market. New Zealanders' experience with cooperative marketing for a wholesale market still has potential for helping underdeveloped countries.

Efficiency and equity in a cooperative factory was made possible by Professor Babcock's invention in 1890 of a test for butterfat content in milk; this enabled suppliers to be paid for quality, not quantity. Further efficiency was made possible by the centrifugal cream separator, especially because it enabled farmers to separate their milk on the farm. Mechanization of dairy factories and mechanization on farms were further advances. But ultimately, it was the determination and industry of the new pioneers that brought about the rapid transformation and remarkable efficiency of the industry. From 1890 to 1935, the dominant characteristic of economic and social growth was the evolution of the closely settled regions devoted to dairy and mixed farming. By then, dairy farmers were the largest occupational group in New Zealand except for various kinds of civil servants.

What makes New Zealand dairying so different from dairying in other countries is that cattle fodder is almost solely derived from pasture, that climate makes it unnecessary to house cattle in winter, and that mechanization has so far proceeded without having to meet the inertia of traditional habits of farm husbandry. The characteristic grassland farming techniques of New Zealand take advantage of the climatic fact that the soil of the North Island, even in winter, seldom gets so cold as to stop nitrogen fixation in the clover nodules of its predominantly ryegrass pasture, so that grass grows all the year round. Short rotation techniques so common in other countries (with high labor costs) are therefore unnecessary. The fact that most of New Zealand's best pastures, whether permanent or long-rotational, are made by grazing stock ensures that higher productivity is gained at the same time as soil fertility is increased.

But the cycle is begun by liberal top-dressing with artificial phosphatic fertilizer. It was therefore of fundamental importance to the growth of New Zealand's grasslands economy that New Zealand in 1919 bought a 16 per cent share in the British Phosphate Commission's concession for working the Nauru Island and Ocean Island deposits of phosphate. Nauru up to 1914 had been German. During the First World War, it was garrisoned by Australian troops. After 1907, the Pacific Phosphate Company had owned the concession, but when Nauru was placed under the mandate of the United Kingdom, Australia, and New Zealand, the Commission was formed with capital from each of the three governments in the proportion 42:42: 16. Although the United Kingdom has the rights to 42 per cent of the output of phosphate in theory, in practice most of it is disposed of to the Australian and New Zealand governments. In 1947, Nauru was brought under the International Trusteeship system of the United Nations, and since then Australia has administered the island on behalf of the other two trustees. New Zealand's twelve fertilizer works produce over a million tons per year of various kinds of superphosphate fertilizers at a very low cost by world standards, which thus keeps down production costs throughout the pastoral and dairy industries. New Zealand's 67 lime factories utilize local materials; methods of extraction and of transporting bulk lime have been so revolutionized that costs have also been held down, to the benefit of the farmer.

Perhaps the most significant modern development in the establishment of high-productivity pasture has been the pioneering of aerial top-dressing. The first test of dropping fertilizer from the air was made in May 1939; more elaborate tests were conducted after the war by the Royal New Zealand Air Force. Private contracting firms began operating in 1949. In 1950, 49,000 acres were top-dressed from the air; in 1956, the figure had risen to nearly 4 million acres; in 1962, over 5½ million acres were aerially treated. Aerial spreading of insecticides, weed killers, rabbit and opossum poisons, and seeds also developed with similar speed. The supply of obsolete, war surplus training planes helped to establish this contracting system.

Top-dressing has made it possible for certain regions of New Zealand (such as the Waikato and the Bay of Plenty) where natural soil fertility is not very high to become the most productive in New Zealand. The New Zealand dairy farmer measures his efficiency by his butterfat production per acre rather than production per cow. Good, well-managed pastures produce from 100 to 150 pounds of butterfat per acre, but some are known to produce 200 to 350 pounds per acre.

Before the advent of refrigeration dairy produce for export was mainly heavily salted butter or certain kinds of cheese. With refrigeration, butter became the more important product, especially when prices rose. Cheese has always been more important than butter in Taranaki and Southland, and butter more important in Northland, Waikato, and the Bay of Plenty. In 1901, about 10,000 tons of butter, 5,000 tons of cheese, and a mere 422 tons of processed milk products were exported. In 1921, just after phosphatic fertilizer had begun to play a large part in pasture establishment, the figures were approximately 44,000, 68,000, and 8,000 respectively. During the twenties, improved pastures, the spread of electric power in rural districts, increased mechanization, and improved efficiency in factory and farming organization resulted in almost a doubling of output. Nearly 100,000 tons of butter, 82,000 tons of cheese, and 6,000 tons of processed milk products were exported in 1931. By this time, over 43 million acres of land were under occupation, and 19 million acres of them were in sown grasses or devoted to annual crops.

The Role of Government: Regulation and Stability

The depression was a heavy blow to New Zealand, but a tremendous increase in butter production enabled the government to meet its international financial obligations. This national integrity was gained at great expense to farmer and urban worker alike, but there is something heroic in the fact (as stated by one economist) that between 1929 and 1934 the dairy farmer received 20 per cent less return than previously but produced five pounds of butter where before he had produced three. For the first time, too, farmers had to face the fact that their unrestricted entry to the United Kingdom market could be threatened. Strenuous protests at British proposals to impose a quota system on imports of butter forced Britain to subsidize dairy production in England, a practice that proved most embarrassing in her negotiations with the European Economic Community in 1962. Beef quotas were imposed in 1934 but did not work satisfactorily. When a levy on imported meat (including mutton and lamb) was proposed instead, opposition from New Zealand and other Commonwealth countries forced Britain once more to institute a direct subsidy for local meat producers.

Farmers became self-righteously indignant at any attempt to destroy free trade principles and turned their suspicious hatred on everyone whom they thought responsible for falling prices—bankers (especially international ones), organized labor (it had been the small farmers who led attempts to break the "Red" Federation of Labour), and the middleman. Extensive experiments with corporative marketing were one result. The muddled theories of Major Douglas' "Social Credit" also caught the imagination of a people who did not understand complex international financial organization. Largely because traditional hostility to urban workers had been blunted by common suffering, Social Credit farmers helped to sweep the Labour Party triumphantly into power in 1935. The day of farmer-dominated government was over. Urban businessmen and urban workers, both very conscious of the pastoral source of New Zealand's prosperity but both concerned with their own welfare, were in future to dominate the political scene.

Labour's policy of planned insulation against international fluctuations included price support schemes for the farming community. The Primary Products Marketing Act 1936 made all dairy produce exported the property of the government ("political piracy," the ex-Prime Minister called this), and a fixed or guaranteed price was returned to the producer based upon prices ruling in the previous eight- to ten-year period. A dairy account was opened at the Reserve Bank (now state-owned), and the experiment of guaranteed prices was launched on a rising market. War brought an extension of government ownership to all other kinds of exported produce and prompted increased government experimenting with methods of stabilization. War also averted much of the threatening conflict over the level of the guaranteed price. Popular readiness to accept hardships in the national cause enabled the government to carry out a wartime policy of stabilizing prices and wages that, despite suppressed inflation, was a considerable success. Bulk purchase agreements with the United Kingdom (which remained in force until 1954) ensured guaranteed prices to farmers and also ensured a surplus in the special reserves that could be borrowed by the New Zealand government to finance other projects. At the end of the war, the withholding of certain of these surpluses while the market was rising caused a great deal of discontent. Price support schemes after the war were designed to meet as far as possible the farmers' true demands for a guarantee against falling prices combined with participation in the benefits of rising prices.

In 1952, the Wool Commission was established to take over the reserves in the marketing account. Although it was originally intended to finance its operations from levies on all wool exported, it has been able to finance minimum support prices from the interest on the original funds. In addition, the reserves have been augmented, and a one-for-one subsidy has been paid to the Wool Board on the 7s. 6d. per bale levied on all wool to finance the research and promotion activities of the Board.

Since 1961, the New Zealand Dairy Production and Marketing Board has acquired and marketed all New Zealand butter and cheese for export and controls other dairy products for export. It also regulates marketing within New Zealand and thus has greatly increased powers in comparison with the Board and the Commission it succeeded. (These two organizations had been formed after the war to take over certain functions of the government's Marketing Department). The Board owns Milk Products (N.Z.) Ltd., a company in England which markets all milk powder from New Zealand, and Empire Dairies Ltd., the chief of the seventeen companies in England that distribute New Zealand butter and cheese. The Board's production and administrative section is financed by a levy on dairy produce, and it shares with the government the management and finance of the Dairy Research Institute. The Dairy Industry Account was exhausted in the 1957-58 season, and the established practice of fixing the guaranteed price at not less than 95 per cent of the previous season's maximum became impossible to maintain. Subsequent fixing of the guaranteed price by the Dairy Products Prices Authority was accompanied by promises of a government loan to finance expected deficits. In fact, only a very small advance was necessary, and the loan was repaid within a year. But the avoidance of an economic crisis by granting government loans to an industry proved to be the beginning of a new technique of stabilization. When a crisis over the price of sugar developed in 1963, it was also decided that the best way to prevent a price rise would be to lend government funds to the marketing organization.

Since 1955, a minimum price system for meat exporting has also been in operation. The Meat Export Prices Committee sets floor prices based on ruling prices during the previous three seasons, modified by considerations such as the ruling prices for other farm products and the general level of costs, prices, and wages within New Zealand. Deficiency payments to farmers are made from the Meat Industry Reserve Account whenever prices paid to farmers are lower than the minimum.

These and other schemes for protecting the productivity and standard of living of New Zealand's farmers have stabilized the industry and emphasized the trend for farming in New Zealand to be conducted like a business, with planned development and orderly marketing arrangements. Nevertheless, wartime scarcity of fertilizer (Nauru was captured by the Japanese during the war), restrictive import licensing (which slowed down the rate of mechanization), and government emphasis during the war on agriculture and secondary industry all contributed to slow down the development of grassland farming. Not until after 1948 was there a distinct improvement. Since then, favorable prices, technological advances, improved scientific research, and government fostering of producer participation in marketing have brought rapid advances. But farmers continue to rail against the rising cost of production, blaming it on the inflationary consequence of the rapid development of protected secondary industry. When the protest is made that New Zealand needs this industry to provide employment, the farmer usually complains that he cannot get labor for his farm. In his mouth and in his spokesmen's mouths is often the ugly phrase "over-full employment." A genuine conflict between those who believe in developing primary industries and those who believe in developing secondary industries underlies the charge. But the "either/

or" analysis is an oversimplification. New Zealand must develop both primary and secondary industries in such a way that all classes in the community will benefit.

An investigating committee in July 1963 reported that in spite of steady increases in production, net farming income had declined between 1957-58 and 1961-62, while the incomes of other sections of the community continued to rise. Lower prices for produce and higher costs, especially sea freights, were the main causes. The rate of capital investment in farming had slowed down, and farmers hoped that government would provide incentives to speed up reinvestment of income, the most important source of new farm capital. Sheep farmers' net income per capita had fallen since 1957, especially in North Island hill country farms, and the slight rise in dairy farmers' income had been made possible by deficiency payments. The return on capital in dairying had been slightly above the return on shares, and the return on sheep farming below. Studies on farm productivity established that in net output from 1920 to 1960 the average compound rate of growth per capita was 2.6 per cent per year. Because exports must increase by about 5 per cent each year to maintain living standards (according to an informed economist), there seems to be some truth in critics' allegations that "a progressive growth economy, with high mass-consumption," has been converted into "a static, even regressive economy." But who is responsible?

The most outspoken critics place the responsibility on urban dwellers. "Townies" are content to allow officials to license all forms of economic activity and so prevent healthy competition and incentive. They allow officials to carry out a policy of encouraging cottage industry instead of full-scale, integrated primary industries (or secondary industries using local resources). They also complacently believe that they enjoy a high standard of living despite the fact that with the money in their pocket they may buy only inferior or costly New Zealand-made goods and a severely restricted range of goods from overseas. In other words, the urban New Zealander, these critics affirm, is a victim of the "cut imports" solution to the balance of payments problem. Nevertheless, some critics also blame the primary producer for not accepting to the full the challenge of the "increase exports" solution to the problem. The producer is content to let powerful monopolies handle his export trade for him. He is interested in his productivity in comparison with other industries in New Zealand but does not pay enough attention to production rates overseas. He is too willing to accept without question his producer board representatives' statements that most available markets have been tapped.

Great Britain as a Market

There is obviously some truth in criticism of primary produce marketing. Only a fundamental change from a century's blind faith in the inexhaustible market of Great Britain can eradicate such complacency. Two major shocks have been delivered to the dairy industry in the past decade, but it is not yet certain that they have roused the producer from his lethargy even in that sector of primary production.

The first of these shocks was a spate of butter-dumping on the United Kingdom market in 1958. New Zealand's protests to Great Britain led to antidumping measures, and after two or three years of sporadic negotiation through GATT, EFTA (European Free Trade Association), and other trade regulating organizations, New Zealand agreed to a new solution that is in many ways revolutionary. For, in May 1963, Britain established a quota system. At the same time as she guaranteed 40 per cent of the market to New Zealand, she eliminated tariffs on non-Commonwealth butter in order to satisfy EFTA demands. Price support programs by highly industrialized nations of their comparatively small dairying industries resulted in dumping on the open market, to the detriment of countries whose dairy industries are basic to their economy; New Zealand farmers hope that these price support systems may be reduced while the quota system lasts and thus allow her eventually to resume her traditional domination of a tariff-free part of the market. It may very well prove, however, that Britain will be able to adjust her own price support schemes to allow her to come closer to the systems favored by the European Economic Community. Thus, the "temporary" expedient for stabilizing the butter market may turn out to be one more aspect of the second shock that disturbed the complacency of the dairy industry and New Zealand as a whole—Britain's application to join the European Economic Community.

When France broke off the negotiations in January 1963, the news was received with relief in New Zealand. The news that Denmark, New Zealand's traditional competitor in the British butter and cheese market, had also withdrawn her application to join the EEC probably added to the feeling of satisfaction. But there can be no excuse for such satisfaction. New Zealand ought to be acting on the assumption that Britain will eventually go into the EEC. The prevailing lack of initiative in looking for alternative markets is officially summed up by the "hope" that Britain will not enter without adequate safeguards for New Zealand's position. The ghost of colonial trust in the "mother" country is still a powerful figure. If Britain and Denmark were to enter the EEC, the expanded Community might even become a net exporter of butter. Even if Britain entered the Community without Denmark, Britain would provide an open market for EEC butter, while Denmark and New Zealand would compete against a 24 per cent tariff, which, with sea freights, would practically ruin New Zealand's trade. The EEC, on the other hand, cannot reduce the common tariff until the common agricultural policy has been implemented. In order to ease the development of a common agricultural market within the Community, a system of levies has been introduced for both internal and external trade. An importing country within the EEC collects a levy on agricultural products from other countries within the EEC equal to the difference in the prices of the exporting country and the prices in its own country. Levies on produce exported beyond the EEC are paid into the Community's common funds. The internal levies will be gradually reduced until prices in all six countries are the same at the end of 1969; the levies on produce exported from the Common Market would be retained. Thus, levies take precedence over all other protectionist measures during the transitional stage. If Britain were to join the Common Market, her price support system would have to conform. Britain's Exchequer in 1960-61 paid out almost as much in agricultural support as New Zealand earned from her total exports. The quota system at present operating for butter may help to stabilize prices and offer chances to reduce subsidies in at least one sector.

New Zealand's appreciation of Britain's difficulties does not obscure the fact that loss of the British market would deal a crippling blow to her dairying industry. Even an effort to reduce production costs to offset a 24 per cent tariff would be vain. EEC tariff on cheese is to be 23 per cent, so there is little point in changing over from butter to cheese, especially as New Zealand's highly organized dairy factories would need a huge capital investment to do so. An effort might be made toward intelligent diversification of the kinds of cheese produced, even though the results may seem futile in comparison with the loss of a bulk market. Most attempts at diversifying the product and its markets have been concentrated on milk powder, condensed milk, and similar milk products, for which there is a potential market in Asia and Latin America. The Philippines and India are at present New Zealand's second best dairy customers, after Great Britain. Competition from Australia is keen, even though New Zealand dominates the British market.

The Need for New Markets

The possibility that Britain will eventually enter the EEC is less of a shock to the meat and wool industries. Wool has for many years gone to a larger number of major customers than has other primary produce, and meat is fast finding more markets as more specialized and diverse products are developed. The EEC already imports more New Zealand wool than does Britain. The U.S.A., Japan, the U.S.S.R., Poland, Czechoslovakia, and China are all considerable customers. New Zealand merely has to participate in the woolen trade's propaganda war against synthetics in order to feel satisfied with her market promotion. The meat industry, however, is forced to get out and sell. It is, on the whole, doing the most impressive job of marketing of all three major industries. Some 83 per cent of all mutton and lamb exports goes to Britain, a fact which demonstrates that New Zealand has gradually, since 1938, come to monopolize the market at the expense of Australia and Argentina. Excellent promotion tactics have opened up a promising secondary market in Japan, and investigation of local taste in mutton and lamb in other countries is gradually leading to variation in the kind of carcass, kinds of cut, and kinds of packaging necessary to develop already existing markets in countries where New Zealand's share is small. Attempts to promote New Zealand meat sales in North America are only in their infancy, and the high standards laid down by the United States for imported meat have somewhat cowed even the most optimistic of promoters. Nevertheless, the United States is New Zealand's major customer for beef and veal. Total exports of beef and veal are still less than half the total exports of lamb and mutton, and other kinds of meat are of minor importance.

It is interesting to note that despite the fact that New Zealand is the largest meat exporter in the world, one third of her production is still consumed within the country. Domestic eating habits could very well be diversified to help an export drive. There can be no doubt, however, that New Zealand is on the threshold of a completely new era of marketing. One might even risk the prophecy that if a third economic shock forces New Zealanders to become involved in this new aspect of economic activity, they will learn fast and succeed even against fierce competition. In the process, a subtle sophistication will become evident in the national character, and hankering in the heartland after nineteenth-century free trade advantages and an inexhaustible market in Britain may be replaced by a more cultivated internationalism.

SEVEN

FROM ADVERSITY TO DIVERSITY

New Zealand today is a mixed economy. Figures of national production for 1960-61 show that farming (agricultural, pastoral, dairy, poultry, and apiarian) accounted for almost half of the total value, mining, fisheries, and forestry for about 7 per cent, building and miscellaneous industries for about 11 per cent, and factories for about a third. What is striking is that since 1938 farming's contribution has decreased by 10 per cent and factories' increased by 10 per cent. Because farming output has kept proper pace with population increase, the development of factory output is all the more significant.

As is usual with any advance in material prosperity in New Zealand, the great expansion of secondary and services industry has been made possible by rising world prices for the products of her primary industries. But deliberate economic policies of successive administrations since 1935 have been responsible for the particular form industrialization has taken. Prosperity has made the welfare state possible, but the welfare state and its underlying philosophy has led to the adoption of certain economic theories that modify considerably the government's overriding concern with the problems of a dependent economy.

The Ideal of Full Employment

Full employment was one pledge with which the Labour Party came to power in 1935. Harrowing experiences of depression transformed the doctrine into a popular ideal, and despite sporadic expressions of dissent, it is still an almost universal national sentiment. Paradoxically, the industries which earn nearly all New Zealand's overseas funds are those least capable of providing flexible opportunities for employment. Dairying in particular is organized in such a way that hired labor is far less important than the labor provided by the farmer's own family. The labor force needed on sheep farms is usually seasonal. Urban secondary industry is therefore the main sphere where the doctrine of full employment may be applied.

The Labour Party's attempt to implement the policy did not require revolutionary measures, for by 1935 the country was already emerging from the depression. The Unemployment Board had been set up as a result of the Unemployment Act of 1930; it was intended to find employment opportunities in private industry, to promote local industries, to establish labor exchanges, to arrange retraining programs, and generally to collaborate with central and local government public works schemes. Adult males were to contribute a flat levy toward an unemployment fund, from which, as it happened, no "dole" was ever authorized. Payment for relief work at subsistence rates was made possible for some of the unemployed during the depression, but as the number of unemployed rose from 11,000 in 1930 to 79,000 in 1933, it was obvious that these measures were inadequately financed and unimaginatively conceived. In 1934, the number of registered unemployed had fallen to 69,000, and in 1935, to 60,000. The Labour Party in 1936 changed the names but not, fundamentally, the functions of the organizations dealing with unemployment. The activities of the Unemployment Board were transferred to the Employment Division of the Department of Labour, and Government Employment Bureaus were replaced by a State Placement Service which operated labor exchanges.

In December 1938, to halt the depletion of overseas reserves and the flight of capital due to capitalist fears of a "socialist" regime, the Labour government issued Import Control and Export Licences Regulations, which were quickly validated by a Customs Acts Amendment Act in 1939. The purpose of export control was to ensure that all foreign exchange earned was sold to the New Zealand banking system; prohibition regulations of 1939 and 1953 were also designed to prevent export of subsidized goods or essential goods that were scarce. Import control has been used for a variety of purposes apart from the main one of preserving the balance of payments and "insulating" the New Zealand economy from external economic fluctuations. Not the least important of these purposes is to maintain full employment by developing, behind a shield of rigorously selective importing, a local market for New Zealand's manufacturing industries. Full employment can be achieved only if there is an unsatisfied demand for local products. When demand is not satisfied locally, and import control keeps it unsatisfied, local enterprise will develop to meet the demand. Such is the theory behind this device for assuring full employment by creating factory jobs. Despite inflationary pressures brought on by such a policy, fast development of certain kinds of industry will follow. Manipulation of import licensing will to a certain extent predetermine the growth of such industry. And government decisions can profoundly affect the precise way in which industry as a whole develops.

Local Manufacturing and Importing

Local manufacturing in New Zealand before 1939 was always in direct competition with imports. It is of course obvious that before the systematic colonization of New Zealand nearly all manufactured goods had to be imported. However, missionary societies were quick to send out skilled artisans such as carpenters, coopers, printers, and blacksmiths to make certain needed articles on the spot. Geographical isolation encouraged enterprising manufacturers to produce consumer goods for the immediate needs of the small and scattered communities which grew up in the 1840s. Even so, for many a decade the most important merchant in each town was the importer, if one may judge by advertisements in local newspapers. On the other hand, high freight rates from England (and even from Australia) provided natural protection for local manufacturers of bulky or weighty goods. Those consumer goods that required close cooperation between producer and consumer could easily compete with imported goods, for specifications sent abroad could so easily be misunderstood or misapplied. And, of course, many perishable goods, especially those using local materials, did not run into competition from imports. Thus, flour mills, flax mills, ropewalks, sawmills, and repair shops of various kinds established by 1845 were followed in the mid-forties by breweries, brickkilns, and cooperages, and in the late forties by lime kilns, ship and boat yards, soap and candle works, and tanneries.

New Zealand by the 1840s had in fact a small export trade in manufactures, mainly in ships and ships' parts. This was made possible by local demand (mostly from enterprising Maoris) for coastal shipping to bring produce to market. But very little is known about the volume of New Zealand's export trade until 1853, when the Australian gold rush was under way. At that time, timber was the major export (£93,000), with wool second (£67,000), and potatoes third (£30,000). Whale oil, grain, and kauri gum were the other principal exports. Manufactured exports were insignificant. Wool and gold in the 1860s accounted for over 90 per cent of all exports. Imports at this time consisted mainly of capital goods for the establishment of local industries but included a remarkably high proportion of consumer goods.

Protectionism

During the latter half of the nineteenth century, especially during the sixties and seventies, ocean freight rates fell spectacularly with the rapid development of the steamship and fast sailing ships. This increased the competitivenes of certain imported consumer goods. But it also helped to establish New Zealand's frozen meat trade, which, after the eighties, ensured prosperity for New Zealand. And prosperity, of course, resulted in a vast increase in the consumption of both imported and locally manufactured goods. Tariffs before the eighties had been low and designed primarily to raise revenue for the Maori wars. In the eighties, they gradually took on a protectionist bias. Even so, the duties were very moderate. The Act of 1888 gave some protection to the manufacture of clothing, boots and shoes, machines, and goods made of brass and iron. Increased protection for some articles in 1895, 1900, and 1921 was in part offset by freeing foodstuffs and other important consumer goods. The moderate system of tariffs that thus evolved up to the First World War probably never offset the fall in ocean freights. To a certain extent, too, tariffs were weighted in such a way as to favor British goods. Thus, local manufactures that thrived were those protected mainly by geography and only to a minor extent by tariff. Growth of local manufacturing was tied to growth of the local market, which in turn grew as a direct result of improved internal communications and transport and vigorous increase in population.

As protectionism developed throughout the world in the early decades of the twentieth century, New Zealand (despite overwhelming farmer support for the doctrine of free trade) was forced to retaliate against what were thought to be "abnormal practices." In 1921, as export prices were collapsing, duties were increased on goods from countries with a depreciated coinage and on goods "dumped" by other countries. The net result was an increase in protection for New Zealand industries, accompanied by a marked tendency to favor British goods. These two tendencies were further emphasized in tariff revisions of 1927, and heavier duties in 1930 underlined the fact that New Zealand, willy-nilly, had been dragged into protectionist practices almost as great as those of any other agricultural or pastoral country. When the United States raised its tariff in 1930, with a special attempt to protect its agriculture, and financial crises spread throughout Europe in 1931, trade restrictions assumed new forms. Import quotas, exchange controls, and the complex tariff systems of the modern world spread quickly.

The British Empire's main answer to the challenge was the Ottawa Conference of 1932. The United Kingdom agreed to continue free entry for Dominion products, to maintain duties on foreign goods, to establish quantitative restrictions on meat imports in an effort to solve domestic difficulties (and competition between the Dominions and foreign suppliers), and to impose new duties on foreign suppliers of certain products such as dairy products and fruit. New Zealand agreed to maintain tariffs in favor of the United Kingdom. The Ottawa Conference was New Zealand's first major attempt to negotiate in an international economic sphere; it confirmed her championship of imperial preference and thus established her as an independent advocate of free trade within the imperial bloc as a second best to world-wide free trade. It did not fundamentally alter her relations with her major trading partners.

Up to the depression of the 1930s, then, secondary industry in New

Zealand received only very moderate protection from tariff. Such protection had very little influence on the rapid development of secondary and tertiary industry, which may more correctly be attributed in the twenties and early thirties to the optimistic vigor and industry of New Zealanders, the growth in working population (helped by immigration), geographical protection (especially shortages during and after the First World War), speed of mechanization, and, probably, improved and cheaper internal transport. But the depression hit industry very hard.

While farmers were increasing productivity phenomenally in a desperate attempt to counter falling prices and contracted income, manufacturing output decreased as a result of reduced domestic purchasing power. A fall in competitive imports was perhaps sufficient to keep most factories going, but at a greatly reduced output. Unemployment was the inevitable consequence, causing yet further reductions in the community's purchasing power. But the effect in a small, optimistic, and energetic country where adversity was usually thought to be within the control of local effort was—and this is not an exaggeration—traumatic. A policy of deliberate insulation of New Zealand's economy from fluctuations in the outside world appealed to farmer and worker alike, and, as it was linked to a policy of full employment, it ushered in the modern era of heavy protection for New Zealand industry.

Postdepression and Postwar Changes

The Labour government's attempts to grapple with postdepression problems by extending the regulative power of government into all kinds of economic, social, and welfare fields was viewed with some alarm between 1935 and 1939, but the coming of the Second World War quieted much of the opposition. Rigid controls were accepted for an all-out war effort that might not have been so easily developed in peacetime. The major form of control was credit control. Through it, the government hoped to stabilize national income, and hence domestic prices, and to redistribute income to provide "social security," at the same time pragmatically bringing about some kind of control of national economic development. The war and its attendant controls vastly increased protection for local industry. At the same time, the number of able-bodied men and women in the armed services and the greatly increased demands on the country to provide food and services for American and other forces in the Pacific left New Zealand with an acute shortage of manpower and womanpower. Human resources were therefore controlled by manpower regulations, which worked in conjunction with conscription for the armed forces. Even at the end of the war, there was such a shortage of employable people that inflation seemed to be a looming problem. Unemployment was seemingly a thing of the past, and industry had to compete for manpower.

The growth during the war years of new industries increased the tendency of manufacturers to rely on imported materials. Import control was especially responsible for the creation of "import substitution" consumer goods industries during the war. Machines, tools, and implements industries, the transport industry (mainly the assembly and repair of motor vehicles), the chemicals industry (especially plastics, paint, and rubber manufacture), though heavily dependent on imported raw materials, all received tremendous impetus. Comparisons between factory production in 1938 and the present are difficult because of a major statistical change in 1951-52, when "heat, light, and power" (i.e., gas and electricity supply) and the logging industry were excluded. But some signs of significant changes of emphasis in industrial development can nevetheless be detected.

In 1938, just over 43 per cent of New Zealand's imports (calculated by value) were producers' materials (including fuels and lubricants and auxiliary aids to production), and just over 26 per cent were consumer goods. In 1951, over 54 per cent were producers' materials, and 20 per cent consumer goods. Since then, the percentage of producers' materials has not fallen below 50 per cent, and the percentage of consumer goods has not risen above 20 per cent. The dependence of New Zealand's industry on imported materials is, therefore, increasing; further analysis shows that the importing of crude and simply transformed materials is increasing at the expense of more elaborately transformed materials. This, of course, reflects an increasing degree of manufacture within the country as well as an increase in the range of kinds of manufacture. But it also suggests that if absolute dependence on imports is to be reduced, raw materials within New Zealand will have to be sought.

As a result of the growth of "import substitution" consumer industries, New Zealand has greatly reduced her dependence on imported consumer goods—much to the wrath of some consumers, who complain of the inferior quality of locally produced articles. But the consumer goods figure of 15-20 per cent of all imports is still very high in comparison with other small countries of high living standards. Until her population grows much larger, however, it is unlikely that the figure can be further reduced. Once New Zealand develops the local manufacture of those foods and beverages which still loom large on the import lists (and this is being done with great speed), the boom in consumer goods manufacture will have reached the end of its first stage. The next stage (which has already begun) will be the consolidation of existing factories and improvement in efficiency and competitiveness with overseas industry, especially Australia's, so that at least some may develop export potential. There are many signs that this development is actually taking place: concern about the increasing incidence of take-over bids and amalgamation of small factories into larger ones, the development of national rather than regional "chains" of consumer goods factories and their outlets, and so on.

As Condliffe has rather severely pointed out, industrial expansion before the exchange crisis of 1957 was largely a multiplication of small workshops, not a factory development in the true sense. Costs of internal transport, the smallness and relative isolation of population centers, and the lack of local raw materials were, he thought, responsible for the fact that most of New Zealand's industrial enterprises cater for the local and not the national market. He presents figures to show how small the scale of operations really was in 1952-53. His absolute figures are chastening for those optimists who foresee a great industrial future for New Zealand. But a healthy trend toward larger factories can be detected even since then. This trend ought to be accelerated if a policy of high productivity and maximum income is to become equally as important as the policy of full employment.

Education for Development

Unfortunately, the nation's extensive experience with small-scale and relatively inefficient manufacturing has helped to prolong unnecessarily the "practical man" mentality so prevalent in all kinds of activity in New Zealand. For example, some New Zealanders still think that trained managers, technicians, and research workers will come out of small, diversified factories. Practical experience, not expensive education, according to such thinking, will cope best with the problems of industry. The urgency for greatly accelerated development of existing industry is not fully understood. The danger in proliferation of "backyard" factories is that habits of thinking and organization adequate for small-scale factory production will be carried over into large-scale factories, with disastrous results. The history of glassmaking provides a good example.

Since 1922, an Australian subsidiary of an English firm has been manufacturing glass and other containers in New Zealand. In 1954, the firm started to produce safety glass in New Zealand to serve the automobile assembly industry. It also commands a considerable share of the New Zealand market in imported window glass. These and associated companies altogether employed in 1963 about 1,750 people, of whom about 1,200 were in glass factories.

In May 1960, a new sheet glass manufacturing company was registered, and in July 1961, a public flotation of £122,500 brought its paid capital to £250,000. A year later, a one-for-one issue at par boosted paid capital to £375,000. The formation of the company and the establishment of its factory in Whangarei were the result of agreements made early in 1960 between the intended company and the government, represented by the Minister of Industries and Commerce. The company had been successful in gaining qualified acceptance by the government of its proposals in competition with the proposals of another New Zealand-owned company, as well as those of the English company and its Australian subsidiary. Government encouragement of the new company undoubtedly resulted from its awareness of the economic advantages of establishing an industry using local raw materials, of providing employment in a region of New

Zealand where lack of opportunity was causing concern, and of saving at least £500,000 per year of overseas funds. To help establish the industry, the government was willing, by import restriction, to provide the new company with up to 80 per cent of the local market, provided that the company would distribute the glass to all ports at a cost-including-freight price at least £10-per-ton lower than the delivered cost of similar imported glass. Another condition of government support stipulated that if an acceptable overseas company, especially one with technical knowledge that might be necessary to the best operation of the factory, should want to participate in the industry, the local company was to agree to such participation but might retain a majority of the ordinary share capital. The company was obliged, of course, to produce evidence that it was technically competent to undertake the production of glass within the economic circumstances laid down.

There can be no doubt that government was reassured by the fact that "overseas experts" were hired, but a chronic optimistic faith in pragmatic experiment to overcome deficiencies in the knowledge of these experts (rather than set up an expensive preparatory research program) was responsible for the difficulties that immediately occurred when the factory began to produce glass in July 1962. An Auckland newspaper reporter transmitted the parochial attitude of the technical management when he boasted that the finer points of glassmaking "had to be nutted out by Kiwis on the spot." He instanced the invention in Auckland "by chaps who had, up till then, been concerned with the carpet-making industry" of the vital glass-cutting process at the end of the manufacturing chain. The locally invented process had turned out to be better than the imported machines, and world patents were being taken out. Nevertheless, the overoptimism of the company meant that more and more money had to be borrowed to keep the factory going while some of the technical problems were being nutted out on the spot by resourceful but untrained Kiwis. The venture was in fact undercapitalized from the beginning, only rudimentary technical investigation was done before the factory began to operate, and intervention by the state was prevented by political considerations. The government agreed in September 1962 to guarantee £80,000 in interim finance and extended the term in November. By December, however, money due to creditors totaled nearly £500,000, of which three fifths was secured. The Australian company offered to take over the going concern on condition that the government approve a price rise of £10 per ton in the factory's product and a ten-year guarantee for its share of the local market, but this offer was rejected because as it later transpired, the firm also wanted a guaranteed 10 per cent return in perpetuity on shareholders' funds. In an endeavor to get on its feet, the company went into receivership. The state-sponsored public accountant appointed by the major creditor—a bank—attempted to rehabilitate the enterprise. He consulted overseas glass manufacturing experts and kept the factory going. When, after a month in receivership, the enterprise continued to lose money, it was decided to sell the glassworks as a going concern. A considerable amount of extra capital and continuity of technical knowledge and experience were absolutely necessary to improve production. By this time, a total of £750,000 had been spent in establishing the industry—a far cry from the initial estimate of £400,000. Protests from a trade union spokesman against the government's refusal to put money into the venture to keep it New Zealand-owned were by this time unrealistic, for technical know-how had proved just as important as capital. In order to get the necessary combination of capital and technical knowledge, the government was forced to make it known that a price rise in New Zealand-made glass (up to 12½ per cent above the delivered cost of imported glass) would probably be necessary to tempt an overseas firm to take over the works.

News of an American company's willingness to take over the works prompted, in May 1963, a last-minute bid by the Australian company (in association with its parent English company) to buy the assets of the New Zealand company for £380,000. This sum was insufficient to enable any payment to be made to shareholders or to unsecured creditors and insufficient to reimburse the government for all the extra money it had put in to keep the factory in operation. The new owners hoped, with the higher price for their product, to have the factory on an economically tenable basis within four years, when they would introduce new equipment to make use of the Pittsburgh sheet glass process. The introduction of this process in addition to the present Fourcault process was to be the occasion for the issue of shares to enable New Zealanders to have partial ownership of the industry. A ten-year guarantee of protection either by import control or tariff ensures 80 per cent of the expanding local market to the industry and possibly will bring about a reduction in the price of glass. The plant was shut down in June 1963 for complete redesigning.

The lessons to be learned from the venture should be taken to heart. The government has since 1962 had a Tariff and Development Board to establish the criteria for industrial development, but this merely ensures protection for the government against backing risky industrial investment and does little to educate those who have the initiative but only imperfect understanding of the research and organization necessary to establish large-scale industry.

One may still be optimistic about New Zealand's industrial future, however. A survey of the history of her power resources, raw materials, and of the industries based upon them that might develop export potential will reveal two things: that diversity of production is indeed well under way, and that vigorous continuance of the trend depends mainly upon the development of her most important resource—human beings. Intelligent management, technical know-how, and efficient research organization even more than capital will lead to low-cost production and high wages as well as full employment. Undercapitalization does not pay.

Efficient Industrial Development

To counterbalance the example of mismanagement in the glass industry, one ought to consider the orderly, successful, and efficient establishment and development of the wood pulp and paper industry in New Zealand.[1]

The two major companies operating in the exotic forests in the hinterland of the Bay of Plenty have different origins. One, New Zealand Forest Products Ltd., developed out of the ruins of a bond-selling afforestation company. It has since taken over the next largest company of the same origins. The combined companies utilize the

---

[1] Condliffe, in *The Welfare State in New Zealand* (London, 1959) gives a succinct and accurate account of the forest industries to about 1957. His access to unpublished material makes the account authoritative.

privately planted forests originated in the twenties by various afforestation companies. The other company, Tasman Pulp and Paper Company, grew out of the preliminary plans for state harvesting of the state-planned Kaingaroa Forest, the largest man-made exotic forest in the world. A combination of state capital and private capital floated the company in 1952. By 1955 it had become a corporation of £6 million capital, with the government retaining a one-third capital interest arising from its ownership of the forests utilized by the enterprise. Since 1959, management and development have been taken over by the Bowater Group, which is entirely responsible for the company's world-wide sales.

New Zealand Forest Products by the end of 1962 boasted that it was the largest New Zealand-owned and operated company, with shareholders' funds of £14 million. It claimed 3,000 employees and fixed assets standing at £16 million. Its forests extended over 200,000 acres, and Tokoroa, its dormitory town, had grown from a few stores and houses in 1947 to a mill town with a population of nearly 8,000.

Tasman by the end of 1962 had a capital of £7 million, which was about to be expanded to £9.7 million by a one-to-ten bonus issue and a £2 million exchange of new ordinary shares with an Australian company representing the two largest individual newsprint customers of the Tasman Company. This arrangement ensured that future trans-Tasman trade would keep the output of the greatly expanded mill at Kawerau working at an economic optimum. Shareholders' funds were about £8 million. The company employed about 2,000 people, and fixed assets were about £27 million. Tasman's forests extend over 260,000 acres, and Kawerau, its dormitory town, has reached almost 5,000 in population.

Thus, it can be seen that the two major companies represent an industrial undertaking of some magnitude. What is remarkable, however, is the speed with which these enterprises became established and the efficiency with which they developed. This was the result of careful planning, thorough research, and wise use of capital, the consequence of the rather unexpected discovery of the value of experiments in the afforestation of otherwise unproductive land. For the planting of areas in the volcanic plateau was partly speculative, partly haphazard, in origin. In 1913, a Royal Commission prophesied that the

Australian gum "may prove eventually almost the most important tree introduced into New Zealand." Up to 1909, only 110,161 of the 40 million trees estimated to have been planted in New Zealand were Monterey pine; 3½ million Australian gums were fourth on the list to larch (11 million), Austrian pine, and Corsican pine (each 3.7 million). Up to the end of the First World War, Monterey pine and the Australian gum were planted at the rate of about 2,000 acres a year, but after the creation of the State Forest Service in 1920 and the postwar interest in private afforestation, planting was greatly accelerated, and 88 per cent of the 636,000 acres planted between 1923 and 1936 were Monterey pine, which proved fast-growing in its new habitat. The dangers of insect and fungal attack on a single-species forest were not fully appreciated until the depression, but so far the vigorous exotic forests have been miraculously free of epidemics. Since 1937, however, planned afforestation has taken such dangers into account and has kept up with research developments throughout the world. Research on particular local problems is perhaps still rudimentary, but at least there is evidence of full awareness of the importance of such research in government and industrial circles. The rapid rise in the economic importance of the forest industries has brought into full public prominence the value of diversifying the future economy of New Zealand by an afforestation policy which benefits both farmers and the community at large.

The forest industries of New Zealand have always depended heavily upon rough-sawn timber as their staple product. Production of indigenous softwood timber has fluctuated between 200 and 300 million board-feet per year since the twenties. The production of exotic softwood timber was about 10 million board-feet in 1921, but the figure doubled by the mid-thirties and had outstripped indigenous sawn timber by the mid-fifties. Total production has more than doubled in forty years.

Much more spectacular has been the increase in pulp and paper production. Pulping of exotic pine logs (no indigenous species are pulped) began very recently. In 1940, only 217 tons of mechanical pulp was produced; ten years later, output had increased a hundredfold. By 1953, chemical pulp was also being produced, on an intentionally large scale to satisfy a long-term contract negotiated with

Australian newsprint manufacturers. Production of pulp products has changed most spectacularly since the first wallboard factory was set up at Penrose in 1941. In 1940, about 6,000 tons of paper and 6,000 tons of paperboard were produced in New Zealand. Fifteen years later, paper production was 22,000, paperboard 18,000, and fiberboard 20,000. Newsprint was first produced in 1955 and totaled 9,000 tons by March 1956. By 1960, there were 89,300 tons produced, along with 52,000 tons of other paper, 39,163 tons of paperboard, and 25,533 of fiberboard. Fine papers are also about to be produced on a large scale.

What is so important about these statistics is that they refer to an integrated industry with flexibly diverse products, an industry in which even by-products and waste products are used as fuels or raw materials for other branches of the industry. And the products of this highly efficient industry are increasingly competing on the world market. There is no permanently protected domestic market, and the Australian market is not an easy one to compete in. Nevertheless, the industry has shown remarkable ability in securing markets, in orderly (even if expensive) expansion of plant, and in planning and executing the necessary reduction of production costs. Mechanized equipment of the finest quality has been installed and is being augmented. Imaginative foresight in employing experienced management and technological expertise and in paying attention to local conditions has contributed to success, although occasional industrial unrest has been caused by lack of experience with the temper of New Zealand labor. Also important has been the careful choice of mill sites, with proper attention to the probable regional development of the Bay of Plenty area.

The Need for Regional Development

Despite the attention of the forest industries to regional development as a result of a surge in economic growth, a Commission of Inquiry set up to investigate access to the port of Tauranga reported in 1963 that New Zealanders in general had an inadequate grasp of the possibilities for regional development. Regional planning made possible through the Town and Country Planning Act 1953 could in fact make the Bay of Plenty and its hinterland a model of a highly diversified region. Three major industries for earning overseas funds already exist in the region: farming, forestry, and tourism. All of them could be greatly improved by integrated regional thinking.

The central volcanic plateau is crowned by three volcanoes (Ruapehu, Ngauruhoe, Tongariro) which are the central attraction of Tongariro National Park. A few miles to the NNE is Lake Taupo. Running through the volcanic plateau to the northeast of this huge inland lake, which is famous for its trout fishing, is the great gash of the Taupo-Rotorua graben, liberally sprinkled with lakes and thermal wonders, which extends to the coast of the Bay of Plenty between Tauranga to the north and Whakatane to the south. The Waikato River, which flows out of Lake Taupo, turns westward and eventually flows northward and westward to debouch in the Tasman Sea not far south of Auckland. The watershed which causes this deflection continues to the north as the formidable Kaimai Range. This mountain chain cuts off the coastal plains of the Bay of Plenty from the rich farming land watered by the Waikato River and by those rivers which flow north into the Hauraki Gulf. The Kaimai Range is traversed by one road (which is being improved as fast as possible), but access to the port of Tauranga is otherwise circuitous. Yet Tauranga is now the fourth port of New Zealand; only Auckland, Wellington, and Lyttelton handle a greater tonnage of cargo. The single railway line which connects Tauranga to the rest of the New Zealand network flanks the Kaimai Range to the north and extends southward along the coastal plain. A proposed tunnel through the Kaimai Range would reduce distances considerably; despite the high cost, it is obvious from a regional viewpoint that it is absolutely necessary. Yet the loss of revenue to the Railway Department and to existing road haulage operators, is seriously put forward as an objection. Both regional and national advantages in lowering costs of production outweigh all such considerations.

Improved access to the port of Tauranga will not only benefit those individual industries which are separately urging the measure but will allow a significant diversification of industries, many of them of potential export value. Costs of production for the farmlands behind the Kaimai Range will certainly be reduced and productivity greatly increased. Moreover, there is still an estimated 667,000 acres of land as yet undeveloped that could be served economically by the port. Much of the hinterland is pumice soil planted with huge exotic forests, and it is only recently that soil survey research workers discovered that the reason for their unsuitability as farmland was simply lack of trace elements, a lack that caused "bush sickness" in cattle and sheep. Since being top-dressed with cobaltized superphosphate and other fertilizers, however, the land has become potentially very productive.

Regional thinking on such matters as improvement of port access will also help to reduce production and transport costs for the new forest industries, even though their sites were originally chosen in full knowledge of what transport facilities were immediately feasible. A more important aspect of regional planning in connection with these industries and with farming is the future establishment and development of secondary industries that will further process their bulk products. The only sign of proper foresight is the Meat Producers Board's cautious proposal to set up abattoirs (farmer-owned and controlled) that could later be developed into an integrated export freezing works. The Board is even more cautious about providing port facilities. Some development of factories to use forest products in new ways has been vigorously promoted in Whakatane, but cautiousness is also to be found in this project because of uncertainty about regional development of transport, power resources, and raw materials of various kinds. Nevertheless, there seems to be more enterprise in these fields than in the third of the potentially most important earners of foreign currency, the tourist industry.

The Tourist Industry

New Zealand complacency about market research in the matter of selling her primary produce is matched by a similar faith that her natural scenic attractions will sell themselves if sufficient publicity is given to them. A touching faith that the producer need only supply the goods is worse than hopeless in tourism, especially because modern transport makes other regions of similar natural beauty just as accessible. Because the Maori people are somewhat unique, their culture is being used to attract tourists. An Institute of Maori Culture at Rotorua has been formed to improve the attraction of Maori custom for the tourist and to develop traditional arts, crafts, and ways of living. This is perhaps a sign that, after a century of uncomplimentary criticism from foreigners, tourist authorities are waking up to the importance of New Zealand's cultural assets. Nevertheless, it will take quite some time to break down indifference to the fact that tourists are more interested in people in their environment than in the environment itself, no matter how beautiful. Gastronomic experiments with New Zealand lamb and mutton, for instance, should be speeded up so that both tourist and exporter may be satisfied at the same time. Aspects of *pakeha* culture could be just as interesting to tourists as Maori culture. Indeed, some tourists are known to gather in city streets at six o'clock on Saturday night to watch the unsavory sight of public bars disgorging their beery customers. This cultural idiosyncrasy is hardly the kind of thing that tourist authorities wish to publicize. But there are many other peculiar aspects of New Zealand life that are of interest to the tourist: an example is the exciting experiments with geothermal steam at Wairakei, which are now part of the tourist itinerary in the thermal region.

Power Resources

Early experiments with test bores indicated the possibility of using the steam in turbines to produce electric power, and subsequent success in so harnessing steam led to concentration upon this type of production. It is obvious, however, that present research with geothermal steam will be of immense benefit when other industrial uses for it are found. Use of steam in the forest industries alone may be of great advantage in reducing costs of production. In the meantime, the technical triumphs in adapting it for electricity have made it one of the few sources of electricity that can be developed fast enough to meet demands of industry within the next few years. The only other source that can be developed with the minimum of delay is natural gas, which was discovered in Taranaki in 1962 in sufficient quantities to make exploitation worthwhile. The Wairakei geothermal power station in March 1963 had an installed capacity of 162,420 kw.—over one twelfth of the total installed capacity of government hydroelectric or coal-burning power stations. Later in 1963, experiments resulted in the successful production of electricity by "flashing" into low-pressure steam hot water that would otherwise be wasted. All these exciting developments take place in a weird atmosphere where the hand of man is as obvious and as interesting as that of nature.

Geothermal steam is one of the most important undeveloped power resources in the Bay of Plenty region. There is also a limited possibility for developing further hydroelectric schemes. The impressive dams along the Waikato River are being supplemented by others on the Rangitaiki River and elsewhere. Investment costs make it imperative, however, to develop only those sites that will produce the cheapest electricity, so that most of the large-scale building of dams is now taking place in the South Island in areas remote from settlement. The largest and cheapest of these is the Manapouri project now under way in the Fiordland area of the far South. It was originally planned to provide cheap power for an aluminum smelter to be established in Southland, but the government subsequently took over the project in order to feed electricity into the North Island grid via a cable to be laid under Cook Strait by April 1965. Because world supplies of aluminum are at present sufficient, the industry will be established to use alumina processed in Queensland only when the economic forecast is more favorable. If it is finally decided to go ahead with the project, a regional plan for Southland will be essential. Experience in the Bay of Plenty might well be of great help. Ineptness in that region may harm future attempts at regional development, the most urgent of which is that connected with establishing an iron and steel industry in South Auckland.

Heavy Industry

Investigation into the technical and economic implications of heavy industry have been made with great care and forethought, and it would seem likely that the same high standards will be maintained as were found necessary for the successful establishment of the forest industries. Nevertheless, a more comprehensive regional plan seems imperative, for the coal and iron sands resources must be exploited in such a way as to produce a maximum diversity of exportable produce as well as a saving in imports of steel. Transport, control of the lower Waikato River (which frequently floods), development of farmlands threatened with inundation both by open-cast mining and by an unruly river, power development, and orderly development of new secondary industry are all intimately bound up with the economic success of the iron and steel industry. The first stage of production is supposed to amount to 150,000 tons of iron and steel per year from 1966, so that the effect on the rapidly developing industrial complex centered on Wiri would be very considerable. Transport proposals range from connecting the Manukau and Waitemata harbors by a canal for barges (a proposal first put forward over one hundred years ago) to increased use of the Tamaki River for bulky and heavy products from new industries, of which merchant bar mills, wire drawing mills, and steel wire rope factories are already in existence. Road and rail development also has to be planned. Parochial pressures now seen to be operating against even such worthwhile planning organizations as the Waikato Valley Authority or the Auckland Regional Planning Authority need to be kept in check. The sad spectacle of parish pump politics operating in South Auckland makes one fear that business and public appreciation of regional planning may not be as great as the present urgent situation demands.

Training

New Zealand is developing and diversifying her industry fairly fast. In the fifties, New Zealand's population increased by about 20 per cent, as did total world population. In the same period, world industrial production increased by 43 per cent and agricultural production by 25 per cent. New Zealand's industrial production increased by 50 per cent. This is not spectacular in comparison with, say, Japan (190 per cent) or Yugoslavia (135 per cent), but it is well ahead of the established industrial nations: U.K. (24 per cent), U.S.A. (30 per cent), or Canada (40 per cent)—all of whom are traditional markets for her primary produce. To keep pace with this development, increased attention has been paid to technical education, despite New Zealanders' characteristic slowness to appreciate the value of all except basic education. For a decade, accommodation and teaching staff have been quite inadequate to cope even with existing demands for polytechnic education. This has led in the last five years to the development of a national and two regional technical institutes that eventually must provide higher technological training for all those who need it. Nor is apprenticeship in New Zealand up to the standard needed for rapid technical progress. In the year ended March 1962, there were registered 5,361 apprenticeship contracts; over one fifth of these were in carpentry, and over one fifth in the motor trades. The only trades other than these to attract more than 200 registrations were coachbuilding, electrical, engineering, plumbing, and printing. The standard of training in most of these trades is not nearly high enough, even though an excellent technical correspondence school gives training supplementary to that provided by the apprentice's master. An examination is compulsory only in the electrical and plumbing trades.

To emphasize the need for greater effort, let us take the example of printing. New Zealand is about to move into the field of fine paper production. Logically, one would expect that book publishing should become one of the country's foremost export industries. But the inefficiency of New Zealand job printing, based as it is on small factories, is such that most printing for all except one large publishing firm is done outside New Zealand. A collection of the letterheads of New Zealand printers is a sad reminder that the typographical art is in the hands of a very tiny section of New Zealand's craftsmen, so that one cannot readily foresee today's apprentices leaping ahead of their masters. It may be hoped, however, that the National School of Printing at Orakei will develop the skill of apprentices as fast and as well as day-release and block-release systems will allow. Scholarships and other incentives have been instituted in the hope that the standards and keenness of the apprentice will be gradually raised. But what of the higher levels of technological training? Where is the imaginative foresight to be found in an industry where techniques are undergoing revolutionary change throughout the world? One seeks it in vain in printing trade publications. The largest and most promising printing and publishing organization in New Zealand is the Government Printing and Stationery Department; its standards of printing and typography are excellent, and it should be possible for large-scale printing and publishing firms using New Zealand materials and New Zealand skill to reach the same level. A boldly planned and carefully guided attempt to build a large-scale, low-cost printing industry in New Zealand might be the best way of ensuring sufficient local demand for the products of the huge machines now being installed at the paper plants on the volcanic plateau. The economically wasteful short runs caused by the demands of a host of small-scale printing establishments in New Zealand will undoubtedly increase the costs of paper production in an industry which must compete with similar large-scale industries in other parts of the world.

It is easy to offer such suggestions, but not so easy to carry them out in a country where individual effort is valued above large-scale, highly skilled, cooperative organization.*

Adversity taught New Zealanders the need for full employment; let us hope that diversity will teach them the need for full employment of all the faculties of their vigorous and adaptable countrymen.

* A case in point is the fishing industry: potentially the only primary industry that could compete with dairying, sheepraising, or meat production on a similar scale, fishing is undercapitalized, ineffectively organized, and woefully decentralized. If other primary produce loses earning power, however, it may become imperative to develop an efficient fishing industry.

```
┌─────────────────────────────────┐
│                                 │
│            EIGHT                │
│                                 │
│      THE OMNIPRESENT STATE      │
│                                 │
│                                 │
└─────────────────────────────────┘
```

EIGHT

THE OMNIPRESENT STATE

The view of New Zealand described in the preceding chapters suggests that fundamental changes are going on beneath superficial advances in material prosperity. These changes will be accelerated if there is any check to material prosperity, such as Great Britain's closer adherence to the European Economic Community or adverse multilateral tariff restrictions on temperate zone primary produce. They will nevertheless continue to occur even without such disasters so long as New Zealanders feel the insecurities of a dependent economy. There can be no doubt that "security" for most New Zealanders does not mean military security or defense. The particular form of democratic civilization to be found in the two largest islands of Polynesia is not simply a local adaptation of nineteenth-century British middle-class civilization; it is an adaptation powerfully influenced by a determined quest for economic security and a humanitarian drive toward social equality. New Zealanders' international efforts since 1935 have been merely an extension of national efforts to achieve an ideal of social security for themselves and, sometimes, for other nations. The main instrument both internally and externally has been the state. Pragmatically calling upon the government to intervene in economic and social matters for the benefit of all, New Zealanders have created for themselves an omnipresent state in the midst of a fundamentally capitalist, free enterprise economic structure.

To the pessimist (a small minority, for expatriation is still possible), "democracy" has become a tremendous pressure, through state paternalism and community opinion, to make the individual New Zealander conform to patterns of living which are the expression of a narrow, comfortable, but nevertheless mediocre materialism. And "civilization" has degenerated into a sophisticated form of a boorish anti-intellectualism and an ostrichlike hatred of the finer forms of art, which, like the products of a free-ranging intellect, tend to disturb, to produce doubt, and even to foment insecurity. New Zealanders, in fact, need to be reminded that

> Security, some men call the Suburbs of Hell;
> Only a dead wall between.

To the complacent, who are undoubtedly the vast majority, New Zealand is the finest place in the world to live in. Any assertion to the contrary will produce the evasive defense that it is the best country in which to raise children. The climate is temperate; extremes of heat, cold, wetness, and dryness are almost unknown. There are few natural dangers—no snakes, no dangerous wild animals, only one or two poisonous insects. The bodily welfare of citizens is well provided for (it is commonly assumed—erroneously—that welfare services in New Zealand are superior to those elsewhere), and there are no extremes of poverty or wealth, no inhumanity of man to man that the state will not correct, no neglect of social services for the less fortunate members of the community. The welfare state in its finest (i.e., its New Zealand) form is the end product of centuries of struggle for social justice. The future is mere conservation and amelioration.

To the optimist who is not complacent, however, the benefits of the welfare state are to be accepted grudgingly, thankfully, or enthusiastically according to individual taste, and the concomitant dangers—complacency, mediocrity, stultification, lack of individual independence and freedom—are to be recognized in order to be overcome. The optimist feels that it should prove possible to have a basic minimum of social and economic security for all and still develop a society that will offer both opportunity for and understanding of the aspirations of those for whom security is not an aim in itself. Indeed, the optimist detects a new spiritual pioneer abroad in a land that until fairly recently was almost completely dominated by the materialist pioneer.

All these sentiments are obviously variations on themes that are propounded in many other modern democracies, but the degree to which the effects of the welfare state are felt in New Zealand is exceptionally high. This is partly because the population is so small and widely dispersed, partly because it is insulated from the rest of the world by a protective network of economic buffers, and partly because national attitudes have hardened unconsciously into an unanalyzed strait jacket for the individual's thinking. Acceptance of government interference is accompanied by an unconscious respect for the "overseas expert" and even, despite public disavowal, by an exaggerated private respect for titled and certificated authority. The easygoing tact of government officials, their high degree of public morality, and their intimate social contact with the rest of the community all make officialdom more acceptable than in countries of greater size or different social values. Analysis of New Zealand's particular variant of the modern democratic dilemma of the individual's rights and privileges in the face of an omnipresent state that truly represents the majority of his countrymen should of course take into account attempts in other modern democracies to strike the proper balance between individual liberty and the legitimate demands of society. Ideally, one would like to be able to compare the role of the state in New Zealand with that of the state in Australia, Great Britain, the United States, and perhaps other British Commonwealth countries. Unfortunately, not enough basic comparative work has been done to allow more than an impressionistic comparison.

The question "Who runs Britain?" was explored in Anthony Sampson's *Anatomy of Britain* (1962). One would dearly like to see a similar anatomy of New Zealand that would allow detailed comparison of the two countries. New Zealand is very like the United Kingdom in that it has an "unwritten" constitution and in that the corridors of power are often to be found in unexpected places. Most conventions and laws in New Zealand are very similar to those in Britain, but there are some that differ remarkably. It is, therefore, unfortunate that the particular kind of responsible journalism that made Sampson's book possible is not yet a tradition in New Zealand.

New Zealand has few truly original institutions, but her citizens pride themselves on the speed with which institutions and ideas originating overseas are adapted for local use. Most are based on English practice, but New Zealand was the first Commonwealth country to adopt the Scandinavian practice of having a government-appointed ombudsman to protect the individual against injustice perpetrated by government servants.

When one examines the traditional sources of power, the gap between prestige and real power, between the dignified parts and the efficient parts, is just as obvious but not nearly so wide as in Britain. The Norris family in Dickens' *Martin Chuzzlewit* has its harmless counterpart in every fragment of what was once the British Empire. In New Zealand, social prestige has been robbed of much of its trappings, however, for since 1947 there has been no equivalent to the House of Lords, and the social activities of the Governor-General have been even more thoroughly democratized than those of the Queen. Despite almost complete statutory limitations on the power of the Queen or her representative, the Governor-General serves an important function in the formation of public opinion. Lord Cobham, for instance, became very popular because he was able to bring elegance and aplomb to the business of interpreting and reinforcing majority opinion, even to the extent of unfairly attacking minority opinions in moral, artistic, and social matters. Sir Bernard Fergusson, on the other hand, will probably play a distinguished part in changing public opinion because his genuine appreciation of Maori culture is helping to spread the proper climate for biracial harmony.

Egalitarianism and the land policies of nineteenth-century governments made a privileged landed class impossible, but an attempt to give social prestige (without true power) to the "squattocracy" still goes on.[1] Despite the growth in recent times of prosperous urban business executives, New Zealand seems amazingly classless. Prestige is indeed divorced from power.

The workings of the efficient parts of traditional governing institutions have become increasingly well known, mainly as a result of the work of the Institute of Public Administration, founded in

[1] A glance through the three-volume, illustrated *Farms and Stations of New Zealand* (ed. G. A. Tait, Auckland, 1957-61) will suffice to show how it continues.

1934, but partly as a result of academic interest in the subject at Victoria University of Wellington. One of the most valuable books on how New Zealand is governed is K. J. Scott's *The New Zealand Constitution* (1962); this book offers the additional feature of comparing—sometimes implicitly, sometimes explicitly—New Zealand institutions, laws, and conventions with those in Britain. Scott emphasizes the high value that New Zealanders place upon the processes of parliamentary democracy. While people in the United Kingdom are becoming alarmed at the gradual reduction of the real power of their proudest democratic instrument, transplantation has seemingly promoted vigor as well as vulgarization, because the tendency for "closed politics" outside parliamentary control to nibble away the prerogative of "open politics" is much less pronounced in New Zealand than in Britain. The smallness of the electorate, close supervision of and attention to parliamentary proceedings (since 1937 they have been broadcast by the most powerful radio station in New Zealand), traditional dependence upon Parliament to embody the public will against private, sectional, or individual will, relative weakness of non-parliamentary pressure groups, pre-eminence of statute law, and a remarkable degree of political awareness and activity among ordinary citizens have all contributed to the retention of real power in the hands of Parliament. Although voting is not compulsory, the average poll at a general election is consistently high, usually about 90 per cent. This is far higher than in the United Kingdom. Psephology is a fast-growing preoccupation of social scientists,[2] whereas general sociology lags behind current achievements in countries of comparable development.

Parliament

The peculiarities of New Zealand's House of Parliament need not be analyzed here, but one or two observations might help to explain why Parliament has retained, even increased, its power in comparison with Parliament in Britain. First, there are only eighty seats,

[2] Cf. R. M. Chapman, W. K. Jackson, and A. V. Mitchell, *New Zealand Politics in Action* (London, 1962). This volume not only analyzes the 1960 general election but also contributes to the understanding of how New Zealand's political institutions are run and what influences are brought to bear on them.

four of which represent Maori electorates. (A half-cast Maori may vote either in a *pakeha* electorate or in a Maori electorate, but it is in practice impossible to enforce any real distinction as to who may or may not register on the Maori roll.) It is possible that Maoris may in the next decade or so decide that separate representation no longer serves any useful purpose, but in the past the system has done much to ensure equal legal rights and privileges for the Maori race. Within Parliament, the caucus (the members of a particular party assembled in private) has great power over deciding party policy and tactics. As Cabinet membership (which is identical in membership with the Executive Council) is normally about sixteen, and the caucus of the majority party is normally between forty and fifty, over one third of the government members of Parliament normally hold positions in the Cabinet. In contrast, a Cabinet of about twenty from among three hundred or more members of the government party forms the top rank of the hierarchy in Britain. New Zealand's system is much more intimate and simpler than Britain's. Nevertheless, convention within the Cabinet is much more complex. In Britain, one government department is normally controlled by one minister; in New Zealand, one minister may be responsible for more than one department, and one departmental head may be responsible to two or more ministers. Ministers do not have their offices in their departments (which are scattered around Wellington in innumerable buildings), but in Parliament buildings. It is thus probable that the state services have a less intimate connection with their political heads than in Britain, just as it is probable that they have a more intimate one with the general public.

The Public Service

New Zealand has its equivalent of Whitehall, of course, but the predominantly British pattern of its bureaucracy has been modified to suit national differences. The Hunt Commission of 1912 called for a non-political, unified, career public service, and the Public Service Act 1912 did a great deal to secure it. Uniform salary scales and other conditions of employment, the entrusting of powers of appointment, promotion, and dismissal to a body independent of political control, and the placing of all departments except the

Legislative Department, Post Office, and Railways Department under this body ensured that an officer could make his career in the service as a whole without being confined to one department and could have his career protected against competitors from outside the service. The Public Service Commission created by the Act was free of ministerial control but responsible to Parliament. The form of the Commission has been altered several times since 1912, but its weaknesses remain: its lack of effective power in all except personnel administration, its lack of a ministerial voice in Cabinet, its absorption in problems of negotiation with the Public Service Association (representing employees) before authorizing changes, and its conflict of responsibility with permanent heads of the 38 departments. Nevertheless, it was largely responsible for fulfilling one of the intentions of the 1912 Act—to destroy "backdoor" or political patronage in staff appointments and promotions and other practices damaging to the creation of a career civil service run by loyal, incorruptible, and politically neutral state servants. And there can be no doubt that New Zealand's state services are indeed models of propriety.

New Zealand's top civil servants do not constitute a special group of mandarins; nearly all have come up through the ranks. A Royal Commission of Inquiry (1962) firmly asserted that in New Zealand it would be impossible to institute direct recruitment of an administrative élite, giving as its reason the country's historical development manifest in the tradition of recruitment from below. Thus, there is no "old boy net," no amateur collegiate tradition, no special class consciousness.

The estimated number of state servants—permanent, temporary, and casual—in 1961 was 111,000 (just under 5 per cent of the population), of whom 62,000 were employed in the 38 departments of state under the control of the Public Service Commission, 25,000 in the Post Office, and 24,000 in the Railways Department. These figures do not include the 29,000 in the teaching service, 23,000 in the hospital service, 12,000 in the armed forces, and 2,500 in the police force. By far the biggest department within the public service, as might be expected in a "young" country, is the Ministry of Works (12,000), with Health, Electricity, Mines, Forest Service, Air, and Agriculture (in descending order) employing over 2,000 each.

The state services in New Zealand differ a great deal from those in the United Kingdom in that many carry out work that their counterparts in Britain merely oversee. Consequently, the New Zealand Health Department is as large as the British Ministry of Health. Departments (not corporations) run railways, generate electric power, conduct scientific research, develop forests, and mine coal. Some New Zealand departments operate like trading corporations in providing life and general insurance, trustee facilities, housing, housing loans, and farm finance. Although Britain has some departments in the trading or servicing fields, a much larger proportion of New Zealand's state servants have this close contact with the world outside the service.

The social legislation of the 1890s brought a proliferation of new state services and an amalgamation of others for more efficient attention to new activities. After 1912, some further reorganization took place. Experiments with public corporations especially for marketing of primary produce, were tried in the thirties, but the accession of the Labour government in 1935 reversed the trend and led to an enormous increase in the size and importance of government departments. In the picturesque language of Bob Semple, the boards were quickly given their "running shoes" in order to bring marketing under direct ministerial control. The public service permanent staff grew from 4,700 in 1912 to over 40,000 in 1962, proportionately a far greater increase than the increase in population. The number of state servants increased at about the same rate as the population between 1910 and 1930, when it stood at 7,800. But an enormous increase occurred during the next three decades: to 11,700 in 1940, 20,000 in 1950, and 38,700 in 1960. Part of the increase was due to progressive reduction in the number of public corporations, most of which had come under departmental control. Indeed, the extension of departmental control during the war resulted in a total of 53 departments. Reduction in the number of departments and the development of semidepartmental corporations after the war reflected the political realities of the time, and administrations since the end of the first Labour government in 1949 have continued to favor creation of corporations bearing strong resemblances to government departments.

The Institute of Public Administration has, since 1934, helped to provide enlightened criticism of the organization of departments of state, both in its *Journal* and, since 1953, in its series of monographs. The controversial *Politics of Equality* by Leslie Lipson (Chicago, 1948) proposed radical changes. But his proposals had surprisingly little effect, probably because they seemed too radical for bureaucrats. Instead, the matter was thought to be more suitable for deliberation by a Royal Commission, which reported in June 1962 and recommended many fundamental changes.

There is little point in analyzing the structure of government administration in New Zealand before the Commission sat, or to describe in detail how it grew, for Polaschek has done this[3] with masterly concision and accuracy. His commonsense, pragmatic approach is so much in tune with the approach of New Zealand's practical administrators that it reveals clearly the difference between United Kingdom and New Zealand philosophies of career service and lends great weight to the authority of his appraisal. But the practical application of some of the academic thinking of the past three decades may also be traced in the Royal Commission's report. The future lines of development may also be foreshadowed in the report, for many aspects of it have already been embodied in legislation.

The imagery of the report shows a change in attitude to administration. The "machinery of government" has been replaced by the organic image of a human body, with consequent concern by the "doctors" for its physical and mental health. The doctors are opposed to "drastic administrative surgery" and recommend mild palliatives and judicious shots in the arm (or other limbs) to bring the organism into adjustment with the changing world of the welfare state and full employment. This organism is not quite well, for its brain (the Public Service Commission) is not in full control of it, and is slightly muddled about the significance of the advisory and administrative roles that the organism has to play. In England, the advisory experts are apparently kept strictly in their place outside the solid core of the bureaucracy (amateurs and professionals, gentleman and players, etc.), but in New Zealand, it seems, the two are not distinguished enough. This is largely because the state service before 1935 was (to paraphrase the solemnities of the Commission's

[3] R. J. Polaschek, *Government Administration in New Zealand* (Wellington, 1958).

report) characteristically a clerk controlled by an administrator, whereas now the state servant is an expert controlled by a manager and coordinated by an administrator.

Financial Institutions

Part II of Sampson's *Anatomy of Britain* is devoted to the financial institutions of the City of London; this was difficult territory to map because of the pervasive secretiveness of the denizens of that part of London and the lack of royal commissions, select committees, and parliamentary debates on their activities. Financial activities in New Zealand are much more open, largely because the credit and currency system is firmly controlled by government. Of the five trading banks, one is state-owned, one incorporated in New Zealand, and three incorporated in Australia. To celebrate the centenaries of their establishment, they have opened their files to historians, so that banking history has recently become fashionable. In April 1956 the Report of the Royal Commission on Monetary, Banking, and Credit Systems threw considerable light on banking practices in New Zealand, and the *Bulletins* of the Reserve Bank provide a great deal of information for economists and laymen alike.

The sovereign right of the Crown (i.e., the government) to control currency and credit has been explicitly laid down by statute since 1960. Both life assurance and general insurance in New Zealand have also been profoundly affected by successful state competition and by state controls. The latest statistical information issued by the Department of Statistics shows increasing state control over hire-purchase and other financial concerns as well.

Government and Industry

Part III of Sampson's book is devoted to the corridors of power in the world of big business. An equivalent survey of New Zealand's managerial structure would reveal that although overseas leviathans dominate some business communities, state corporations are usually more important, and in some fields (such as forest products, insurance, and brewing) local corporations are formidable rivals. The three great British corporations—Shell, Unilever, and ICI—are well established, and British automobile manufacturers have a protected market against the larger American firms. Five of the seven sisters of the oil world fight their international battle out on New Zealand soil, but Shell and British Petroleum have the upper hand. Only six oil companies operate in New Zealand, and although all six are represented in the New Zealand Refining Company, Shell is the largest shareholder. This giant new refining company is building and will operate an oil refinery at Marsden Point, Whangarei (in the North Auckland peninsula), which is planned ultimately to meet most of the national demand for petroleum products. Although the new corporation will be one of the decentralized leviathans, state sponsorship of its establishment, development, and operation will ensure that the state will remain a potent force in the background. Such state regulation of industrial development is a marked characteristic of New Zealand life.

Government intervention in industry (usually by representation of the Treasury or the Department of Industries and Commerce on the board of directors) has become an accepted procedure for the flotation of large-scale industries using state-owned raw materials. The most obvious examples are the Tasman Pulp and Paper Company Ltd. and what is now in effect a subsidiary, the Kaingaroa Logging Company Ltd. It is also an accepted procedure that government participation is reduced once the corporation so formed is standing on its own feet and operating for the good of the nation as well as of its shareholders. For instance, the government held shares in the British Petroleum Company of New Zealand Ltd. from 1946 to 1955. The cross-fertilizing influence of civil service and corporation administrative and organizational methods in such large-scale ventures makes it very difficult to detect any real difference between a state trading and service organization (whether a department or a corporation) and a large-scale private enterprise concern. Cynics say that the only difference between some private corporations and a government one is that the government one makes a trading loss.

Nevertheless, the uneasy position of the nationalized industries in England, especially the national utilities (coal, gas, railways, electricity, and airways), has only a faint echo in New Zealand. The main cause of the uneasiness in Britain is that most of the industries were nationalized in the years 1946-47, causing a very large lump in the neck of the boa constrictor. In New Zealand, state operation of coal mines began as long ago as 1901. Even with vigorous development in the next decade, state mines never exceeded 15 per cent of total production. During the Second World War, the state bought all except three large private mines and became responsible for 50-60 per cent of the total output. In effect, the 36 mines now in operation are equivalent to a nationalized industry, since the main consumers of coal are the railways, which have been state monopolies since early in the century. State-owned lines in 1880 already totaled 1,182 miles, so the take-over of private lines created no administrative problems. Gas in New Zealand is still privately owned or run by local bodies, but the discovery of natural gas in Taranaki may lead to changes in the system of ownership, because the main customers will probably be in South Auckland. Most electricity in New Zealand is generated by government-owned plants. A shortage of electricity led to an attempt to coordinate electricity and gas supply in the 1950s, but since 1956, gas undertakings have been kept going and expanded by subsidies and grants from a Gas Industry Account administered by the New Zealand Gas Council. Such pragmatism means that state operation of the nationalized industries has not suffered the growing pains that have cramped the British industries. Instead, there is a bewilderingly complex system of administration in New Zealand, which seems to work, but with what efficiency few can tell.

Indeed, the problems of operating nationalized industry at a loss for the sake of fair treatment of customers and to keep monopolies from falling into private hands has led in New Zealand to a complacency about efficiency which is somewhat alarming. The major worry is, of course, the railways, as in Britain. But in attempting to keep these essential services from running at too great a loss, government controls over road transport and other competitors may be retarding rather than improving the transport system of the country. All the complications of transport licensing are an extra burden on taxpayers, and it becomes increasingly difficult to assess the actual efficiency of the complicated transport system in New Zealand. However, there are signs of increasing competition with the state monopolies, for private air services (after duly being licensed) have since 1951 been competing with as well as supplementing the National Airways Corporation (the state monopoly operating from 1946-47). Attempts to sell National Airways to a private corporation have failed. It is ironic, however, that one of the major private companies (financed largely by Australian capital) has recently been asking for financial support from the government.

Without going further into the complex set-up of foreign, state, and local corporations, it should be fairly obvious that New Zealand has had considerable experience in state enterprise that will continue to influence all forms of highly organized private enterprise. This is especially obvious when one notices that a large proportion of the managerial personnel of the big new forest industries were trained within the New Zealand State Forest Service, and that the greater portion of all industrial, agricultural, and scientific research in New Zealand is done within government departments and the results made available to industry and farmers.

Professions in Industry

The managerial revolution has not led in New Zealand to the scramble for managers so obvious in other, more industrialized countries, but there are definite signs of a growth in the executive class since the Second World War. Even more obvious is the growth of businesses that depend to a large extent on the businessman's expense account—restaurants and motels, for instance. The advertising columns in the newspapers are not full of blandishments designed to attract managers. But they are full of large advertisements calling for qualified accountants. Most managers in New Zealand come up from the ranks, but aspirants find that professional training as an accountant is an important qualification. Accountancy has been taught in the universities for quite some time and on a scale quite foreign to British traditions. The universities conduct professional examinations for membership of the New Zealand Society of Accountants as well as for the degrees of Bachelor of Commerce and Master of Commerce. Part-time study in the past has enabled budding accountants and managers to "improve" themselves as they gain practical experience, but with the trend toward more full-time study, Commerce degrees are being reorganized to provide administrative as well as accountancy training. A new concept of management may well be on the way.

The future of engineers in the community is also bound up with trends in university education. Membership of the various institutes—mechanical, electrical, chemical, or civil—is prized but not attended with the same importance as in Britain. The New Zealand equivalent is the New Zealand Institute of Engineers. There is still a strong tendency to invite "overseas experts" for consultation on major projects, and because the main employment opportunity for most engineers, scientists, and even architects is still the state service, the importance of the professions is not adequately understood. The low salaries paid in comparison with other countries is a fair indication that they have not acquired the prestige of their counterparts in Britain or elsewhere. Indeed, so pervasive is the influence of the state that even the salary structure of the professions seems to be fixed by custom in relation to salaries paid within the state services.

The Role of Unions and the Arbitration Court

Sampson, in the endpapers of *Anatomy of Britain*, attempted to symbolize the Establishment of England by drawing a cluster of interlocking circles of various sizes. Each represented a group of people who wield power in Britain today, people who are preoccupied with their own expertise and who, because of characteristic secretiveness, are linked with people in other circles only by the slenderest of threads. One cannot avoid surmising that a similar symbolic representation of the Establishment in New Zealand would be dominated by a large circle representing the state services. Most of the other circles of the British Establishment would also be included, but in different sizes. One circle at least would have to be added—that representing the Arbitration Court. For, despite certain similarities with the Australian system, New Zealand's conciliation and arbitration machinery probably constitutes her most original contribution to the theory and practice of the welfare state. It probably also expresses to a remarkable degree (and certainly helps to mold) characteristic national attitudes to life.

The Registrar of Industrial Unions is empowered by the Industrial Conciliation and Arbitration Act to register any society of employers of three or more members, any society of workers of fifteen or more members, or any society of workers containing not less than 25 per cent of the total number of workers engaged in a particular industry within a particular industrial area. Registration is voluntary but brings with it certain restrictions and controls. The union is legally bound to follow certain rules laid down by the Act, ensuring that officers may be elected or removed by secret ballot, that meetings are conducted in a prescribed democratic manner, that the powers and duties of union officers are specifically limited, that industrial agreements are made and executed in specified ways, that the roll of members is maintained and purged according to certain procedures, and that certain controls are placed upon property and funds, including an obligation to keep and audit proper accounts. To a certain extent, the imposition of subscriptions and levies is also controlled. Registered unions must furnish an annual return showing the number of their members and other information about their activities. But perhaps the greatest restriction is that by registering, a union loses the right to strike or stage a lock-out. On the other hand, a union of workers gains the right to compel employers to negotiate with it to make an industrial agreement, and, conciliation failing, to obtain from the Court of Arbitration an award laying down minimum wages, hours, and working conditions which will apply within the industrial district to all workers in the industry. Unions of employers frequently seem to think that the only advantage in registration for them is self-protection against demands of the workers' unions, for they have no right to compel an unregistered union to conciliate. Nevertheless, the main benefit to them is industrial peace.

Although registration under the Act entails forfeiting the right to strike, most workers' unions in New Zealand are registered. Those who prefer to keep their right to "collective bargaining" and the right to strike are, however, limited by the Labour Disputes Investigation Act, originally based on Canadian practice. When a party to a dispute involving a society not bound by an award or industrial agreement wishes to stage a strike or lock-out, it must give formal notice to the Minister of Labour, who will refer the dispute either to a public servant called a Conciliation Commissioner, whose duty it is to call a conference of the disputing parties, or to a labor disputes committee for investigation and recommendation. If no settlement results, the Registrar of Industrial Unions may conduct a secret ballot of members of the society to determine whether the conference's or committee's recommendation be adopted or a strike or lock-out be called. Seven days' notice (the "cooling-off" period) must be given before either action can be taken legally.

Thus, the right to strike against an employer or the employers' right to stage a lock-out is forbidden for a large proportion of New Zealanders and severely limited for the rest. The New Zealander's conditions of work, his wages, and his hours of work are laid down by a complex system of awards and general wage orders by the Court of Arbitration, complemented by industrial agreements of various kinds negotiated through conciliation machinery. These are supplemented by statutory legislation of the normal kind, which is further complicated by the fixing of wages and conditions by various tribunals, such as those dealing with state services, railways, and post office, the waterfront industry, and so on. Yet, foreigners frequently misunderstand how the system works and tend to think of the system as being more restrictive than it actually is in practice.

The Court of Arbitration has two functions—legislative (the promulgation of awards, apprenticeship orders, and so on) and judicial (the interpretation and enforcement of industrial laws, whether statutory or as established by industrial agreements and awards). The Court consists of a judge, who must be a barrister or solicitor of not less than seven years' standing (in every way equivalent to a member of the Supreme Court), a member appointed on the recommendation of the industrial unions of employers, and a member appointed on the recommendation of the industrial unions of employees. A Registrar of the Court completes the panel. The Court in its legislative capacity acts as the final arbiter on disputes referred to it by councils of conciliation convened by a Conciliation Commissioner.

The Conciliation Commissioner presides over a conciliation council in which the two sides are represented by an equal number of assessors. The two sides must reach agreement among themselves, for the Commissioner has no vote. If they do agree, the consequent agreement may be filed with the Clerk of Awards or referred to the Arbitration Court to be issued in the form of an award, a course usually preferred because an award of the Arbitration Court covers the whole industry and not just the conciliating party. If conciliation fails, the points of the dispute have been so thrashed out in discussion that it speeds the Arbitration Court's work of deciding on the terms of the award that should be promulgated. These awards are normally current for a maximum of three years and normally may not be amended during currency unless all the original parties desire a revision. General orders amending the rates of remuneration in all awards and agreements may, however, be made by the Court under the Economic Stabilization Act, and such general wage orders in the past have been the keystones of wage stabilization as practiced in New Zealand.[4]

Statutory legislation governing industrial conditions and relations before the Factories Act of 1894 was almost wholly a cautious imitation of legislation previously enacted in more industrialized countries, with a largely unperceived but increasing delegation to the state of regulatory powers for the sake of expediency. Expediency was almost certainly the major motive for the development of conciliation and arbitration machinery, too. The widely scattered, embryonic forms of the most active of workers' unions had received an unexpected setback when they pitted their uncertain strength against their employers in the maritime strike of 1890, which began in New South Wales. Public sympathy for the strikers was seemingly alienated when the strike nearly spread to the government railways, but the employers' harsh refusal to negotiate or arbitrate with the watersiders and miners stirred the public's latent humanitarian desire for industrial harmony and a "fair" wage. This desire had arisen as a result of the antisweating movement of the previous decade—a genuinely popular revulsion against allowing in the new Utopia the worst and most scandalous aspects of the industrialism of the older countries. Fortuitously, extension of the franchise (manhood suffrage, 1879; abolition of plural voting, 1889; adult female suffrage, 1893) enabled the humanitarian

---

[4] The history of the Arbitration Court is admirably if somewhat austerely told in N. S. Wood's *Industrial Conciliation and Arbitration in New Zealand* (Wellington, 1963), and its importance for economic history brilliantly summarized in Condliffe's chapter "State Regulation of Wages" in his book *The Welfare State in New Zealand*. The social, economic, and political forces which led to its creation are expertly analyzed by William Pember Reeves in his *State Experiments in Australia and New Zealand* (London, 1902). We may therefore concentrate here upon those aspects of the history of conciliation and arbitration that seem to reveal uniquely the temper of New Zealanders.

indignation at the exploitation of women and youths and the frustrated working-class aspirations to be channeled directly into the political arena. The 1890 strikes brought in their train a damaging blow to the growth of unionism. New Zealand trade unionists pinned their faith on parliamentary action to establish compulsory state machinery to strengthen unionism.

Conciliation was at first maimed by employers' hostility to it and by workers' fear of victimization if they took part in the proceedings. The conciliation system was saved in 1908 by the enactment of the principle of unanimous recommendation. One of the major difficulties in the original Act of 1894 had been the principle of simple majority for reaching an agreement. Thus, opposing assessors spent a great deal of their energies in gaining the casting vote of the chairman instead of negotiating with each other. By denying the chairman a vote and insisting on unanimous agreement, the 1908 Amendment Act resulted in a perceptible rise in the percentage of industrial disputes actually settled in conciliation. In the meantime, however, the Court of Arbitration had gained an ascendancy that improvement in conciliation could not overtake. And the reason for this ascendancy was undoubtedly the New Zealander's desire for protection and uniformity. The quest for security brought in its train a strong desire to have any achievement protected and safeguarded, and the Court of Arbitration became the great bulwark. Court awards spread the fair wages granted by good employers throughout the whole industry in their particular industrial district and brought poor employers up to minimum requirements. Employers, on the other hand, were on the whole very pleased with the results; no strike occurred in New Zealand from 1894 to 1906. One must not underestimate the extent to which employers in New Zealand shared the benevolent humanitarian attitude that is a striking national characteristic of the period.

The Court received the kudos for what was in effect the result of a buoyant economy. But economic difficulties and delays in the Court that resulted from side-stepping the conciliation machinery soon brought increasing dissatisfaction among workers' unions. Anti-arbitration sentiment helped to strengthen the growth of the first Federation of Labour (the "Red Feds," as the farmers called its members), which believed in collective bargaining. A 1913 strike was the culmination of seven years of sporadic industrial unrest, and its defeat (and the extinction of the Federation) precipitated the Labour Disputes Investigation Act and completed the conciliation and arbitration system which so clearly expressed the national desire for protection, solace in restrictive conformity, respect for order by decree, faith in the benevolence of the state as well as desire for industrial harmony, and freedom from militant unionism. For the second time, self-reliant unionism suffered. The growth of the New Zealand Labour Party, however, seemed to offer alternative political channels for working-class aspirations.

The Arbitration Court, following the lead of Judge Higgins of Victoria (Australia) in the famous Harvester Award of 1907, began a significant departure from its "fair wage" policy toward wage-fixing on the basis of safeguarding a specific standard of living. Basic wages for three classes—skilled, semiskilled, and unskilled—and cost-of-living bonuses based upon current estimates of the rise or fall in cost of living were increasingly promulgated and written into awards when they came up for review. Social security was winning its way, probably at the expense of direct negotiation between employer and workers. The Court in fact slowly and steadily developed its protective rather than its conciliatory role. Its power to safeguard standards for workers was such that it proved too inflexible to cope with violent economic fluctuations, and thus, panicking employers turned against it during the depression. An Act of 1932 almost destroyed the Court's protective powers. Although the Act was designed to please hard-pressed employers, it was too late to be effective and succeeded only in creating deep bitterness in the trade unions. The threat to industrial harmony and the widening of the gap between employers and workers that the depression produced made most thoughtful employers wish to see awards and industrial agreements restored. When the Labour Party came to power in 1935, it swiftly restored the standing of conciliation councils and the Court of Arbitration.

Paradoxically, Labour's 1936 Amendment Act both strengthened and weakened the unions. National unions were legally permitted for the first time (previously, a union could operate only within one of the industrial districts) and compulsory unionism established. The gradual and steady shift of function of the Arbitration Court from mediation to protection was strengthened, but self-reliance in the unions was weakened. Increasing use of the Court to implement stabilization policies of the government during the Second World War led to some erosion of the workers' share in the results of national productivity and partly accounted for the rise of militancy on the waterfront and elsewhere. A practically separate conciliation and arbitration system was set up to deal with industrial matters on the waterfront, but discontent continued.

An Amendment Act of 1939 had increased the power of the Minister of Labour to deal with infringements of the Act; specifically, he was given the power to deregister a union that struck illegally and to register a new one. This power was exercised in 1949 in a dispute involving a carpenters' union. The Federation of Labour's recognition of the newly registered carpenters' union widened the gap between unions that supported the arbitration system and those that believed in collective bargaining. Other divisive issues finally led to the creation of a militant Trades Union Congress in 1950. Unrest on the waterfront culminated in the third and greatest major strike in New Zealand history—the watersiders' strike of 1951. For the third time, self-reliant unionism (somewhat overconfident and irresponsible through lack of tradition) was crushed. This time, the harsh retaliatory measures included deregistration, registration of a new union, and new restrictive legislation that alarmed some people because of its effect on civil liberties.

There can be no doubt that the government acted in full confidence of national approval and even union approval of the conciliation and arbitration system, but the danger to individual liberty (apart from the rights of the small group of leaders it was designed to defeat) went unnoted except by a small minority. Official and public satisfaction with the comparatively strike-free decade that followed is combined with a remarkable complacency about the kind of statutes that may be established in the name of law and order.

The same kind of complacency still operates in such matters as censorship of books. However, the speed with which legislation has been placed on the statute book in recent years has increased the demands of responsible citizens for the reconstitution of a second chamber to the House of Representatives. A petition signed by 13,489 people requesting a written constitution and a second chamber was laid before Parliament toward the end of 1961. Nevertheless, it is probably true that because the omnipresent state is a benevolent one, New Zealanders are often unaware of the dangers implicit in the tremendous powers that they have given to it. But non-New Zealanders are also often unaware of how much actual control of the vast organization remains with the general public. As the population grows, and the economy diversifies, the character of the state will change. But deeply ingrained in the national character is pride in the working democracy made possible by a very small community that has learned to lean heavily on the protective power of its legislature. And when due allowance is made for the usual grumbling that is inevitable wherever authority bears down on the individual, New Zealanders are both proud and constructively critical of their state service.

International Relations

If we return briefly to New Zealand relations with the rest of the world, we must base our future hopes on the abilities of the state servants in the External Affairs Department. Recruitment to this department since its foundation in 1943 has been of a very high standard. If we may judge by the quality of the essays in *New Zealand's External Relations* (ed. by T. C. Larkin, Wellington, 1962), twenty years' experience has produced thinking of high caliber. Civil servants may in fact be more enlightened and advanced than their political chiefs and the public whom they serve. Therefore, one would expect that any real initiative by New Zealand (as distinct from attempts to fulfill conscientiously a recognized international obligation) would normally be an enlightened but cautious attempt to interpret the will of the community. In other words, original international activity will continue to be an expression of fundamental national values.

It is very interesting to note that when A. D. McIntosh, in his essay on administration of an independent foreign policy, wished to illustrate New Zealand initiative, he cited the example of the despatch of £5,000 worth of educational supplies to Laos. There is no doubt that New Zealanders value basic education; because it has ensured prosperity for their own community, they generally believe it to be essential for other communities. It is perhaps significant that the first Maori renaissance in the early part of this century was led by Maoris who had faith in certain aspects of *pakeha* education, especially in the fields of health and elementary education. But it may be of equal significance that the new Maori renaissance is being led by men who value technical and higher education. In 1961 a Maori Education Foundation was set up to help Maoris overcome disabilities caused by a cultural background different from the culture of those for whom the general system of education is designed. In appealing to the good will of Maori and *pakeha* alike, the drive for funds has made the general public more aware of the needs of a minority culture and at the same time has made the value of that culture more widely understood. The motive behind the Foundation—to maintain racial harmony by ensuring that Maoris are equally well prepared by education to compete with *pakehas* for employment in an urban environment of the future—is a sound one. A similar effort for education in the Pacific islands may be just as urgently needed.

New Zealand already spends a very large amount every year on basic education and on health services in the islands. Responsibility rests equally upon two government departments, the Education Department and the Department of Island Territories. The latter is hampered by lack of highly trained educationists and economic advisers, although much well-intentioned work has been done, especially in recent years. The basic education provided is as good as a pragmatic approach to the peculiar difficulties allows. The good will may be measured by the fact that 171 New Zealand teachers are at present supplementing about 5,000 local teachers in the islands. But when it is realized that the primary school population is 132,000 and the secondary school population 13,035, it would seem that greater effort is needed in providing advanced technical and higher education. At the moment, only 200 students from the islands are receiving more advanced training in New Zealand schools, trade training centers, and universities. Another 200 from islands not administered by New Zealand are also being assisted and supervised in New Zealand. New Zealand is not parsimonious about education and health in the South Pacific, but more fundamental thinking about her obligations would ensure that the money was spent in a more effective way. Some progressive thinking is already being done within the state service, but state servants must await community sanction. A study of the field of education would establish that New Zealand has fallen down badly in comparison with Australia. Australia is already planning a university for New Guinea that will act as a focal point for Melanesian and Oceanic advancement. New Zealanders should have listened before now to proposals to establish a university in Western Samoa or in Fiji (to include the Central Medical School). Such a university would act as a focal point for educational advancement in the Pacific. Lack of thought in this field is not merely hampered by following Australia's lead instead of acting independently; development within New Zealand of a proper respect for technical and higher education is too recent. External activity is, as always, a measure of internal development. New Zealand is still, unfortunately, best adapted to develop and maintain in health the physical nature. There are, nevertheless, signs of stirrings in the educational field that promise a coming effort to develop and maintain in health the intellectual nature of her citizens. When this effort is extended into external relations, it will no doubt be of enormous benefit to her nearest neighbors, and New Zealand may genuinely earn the title of a Polynesian Power.

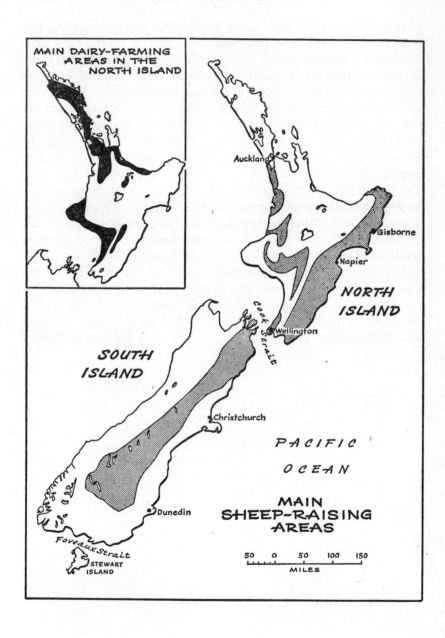

MAIN DAIRY-FARMING
AREAS IN THE
NORTH ISLAND

Auckland

Gisborne

Napier

NORTH
ISLAND

Cook Strait

Wellington

SOUTH
ISLAND

Christchurch

PACIFIC

OCEAN

MAIN
SHEEP-RAISING
AREAS

Dunedin

50   0   50   100   150
MILES

Foveaux Strait

STEWART
ISLAND

Recommendations for reading have been incorporated into the text and footnotes of the book itself. This short survey is intended to select and supplement those recommendations in a more convenient form.

An official government publication, *New Zealand Official Yearbook* (68th issue; Wellington, 1963) is a mine of information about New Zealand, especially if compared with earlier issues. The shortest and most comprehensive official publication that gives both an historical and geographical survey of New Zealand is *A Descriptive Atlas of New Zealand* (ed. A. H. McLintock; Wellington, 1959).

F. L. W. Wood's *New Zealand in the World* (Wellington, 1940), was long the only book to deal adequately with New Zealand's international ties. B. K. Gordon's *New Zealand becomes a Pacific Power* (Chicago, 1960) is an American attempt to fill the need for an historical assessment of New Zealand's foreign relations. A distinguished collection of essays by those who have helped to shape foreign relations was edited by T. C. Larkin and published as *New Zealand's External Relations* (Wellington, 1962).

No comprehensive history of the forces shaping New Zealand in the nineteenth century has yet superseded William Pember Reeves's *The Long White Cloud: Ao Tea Roa* (4th ed., with additional chapters by A. J. Harrop; London, 1950). A number of good short histories may be consulted for both nineteenth- and twentieth-century influences. J. C. Beaglehole's *New Zealand: A Short History* (London, 1936) is the most distinguished of the earlier ones. The most influential textbook on the subject has been J. B. Condliffe and W. T. G. Airey, *A Short History of New Zealand* (9th ed.; Christchurch, 1960), a concise history that has been constantly revised since it began in 1925 under the sole authorship of Condliffe. The most readily available and up-to-date examples of the "short history" are Keith Sinclair, A History of New Zealand (Harmondsworth; Penguin Books, 1959), and W. H. Oliver, The Story of New Zealand (London, 1960).

Maori history is still firmly based upon two indispensable books by Sir Peter Buck (Te Rangi Hiroa): Vikings of the Sunrise (Christchurch, 1958; first printed in New York, 1938), and The Coming of the Maori (Wellington, 1949). Traditional accounts of the settling of New Zealand have been called in question by Andrew Sharp in Ancient Voyagers in the Pacific (Wellington, 1956), rewritten as Ancient Voyagers in Polynesia (Auckland, 1963). The best histories of individual tribes are John Te H. Grace, Tuwharetoa (Wellington, 1959), and L. G. Kelly, Tainui (Wellington, 1949).

The economic history of New Zealand is most fully covered in two books by J. B. Condliffe that also touch on social and political history: New Zealand in the Making (London, 1959), and The Welfare State in New Zealand (London, 1959). A more detailed and abstract study of economic cycles in New Zealand up to 1914 is C. F. G. Simkin's The Instability of a Dependent Economy (London, 1951).

Intellectual and cultural history is largely confined to the field of education. J. C. Beaglehole's The University of New Zealand: An Historical Study (Wellington, 1937), is the most rewarding book, but other publications of the New Zealand Council for Educational Research have specialized information of great value. A. G. Butcher's Education in New Zealand (Wellington, 1930), is a careful but rather plodding book that contains a great deal of factual information about the growth of the education system.

The following anthologies have been selected to serve as useful reflectors of national feelings and ways of life: Desmond Stone, ed., Verdict on New Zealand (Wellington, 1959); Landfall Country (ed. by Charles Brasch; Christchurch, 1962); An Anthology of New Zealand Verse (ed. by Robert Chapman and Jonathan Bennett; London, 1956); The Penguin Book of New Zealand Verse (ed. by Allen Curnow; Harmondsworth, 1960); and New Zealand Short Stories (ed. by D. M. Davin; London, 1953).

Geographers have so far contributed most toward growing awareness of cultural regionalism. K. B. Cumberland and J. W. Fox, New Zealand: A Regional View (Christchurch, 1958) is the most thorough and comprehensive book on the subject; B. H. Farrell, Power in New Zealand: A Geography of Energy Resources (Wellington, 1962) is the first of the more specialized studies that will undoubtedly grow out of general studies. A. H. McLintock, A History of Otago (Dunedin, 1949), is the best of the provincial histories. H. C. D. Somerset, *Littledene: A New Zealand Rural Community* (Wellington, 1938), and W. J. Campbell, *Hydrotown* (Dunedin, 1957), are pioneering sociological studies of great interest. H. Guthrie-Smith, *Tutira: The Story of a New Zealand Sheep Station* (3rd ed.; Edinburgh, 1953), provides great insight into the life of what has been called the "heartland" in my chapter on regionalism.

The nature of Maoritanga may be most easily inferred from the pages of the quarterly journals *Te Ao Hou* (Wellington), a government publication, and *The Journal of the Polynesian Society* (Wellington). Sir George Grey's translations of Maori legends have been reprinted as *Polynesian Mythology* (Christchurch, 1956).

For fine insight into New Zealand's pastoral economy, one cannot do better than read Sir E. Bruce Levy's *Grasslands of New Zealand* (2nd ed.; Wellington, 1955). Perhaps the most useful guide to the development of industries other than the pastoral is *New Zealand's Industrial Potential* (ed. by R. G. and M. W. Ward; Auckland, 1960).

The government and public administration of New Zealand is analyzed in a number of publications of the Institute of Public Administration, of which the most useful is probably R. J. Polaschek, *Government Administration in New Zealand* (Wellington, 1958). It should be read in combination with Leslie Lipson, *The Politics of Equality: New Zealand's Adventures in Democracy* (Chicago, 1948). An early analysis of great value is William Pember Reeves, *State Experiments in Australia and New Zealand* (London, 1902). L. C. Webb, *Government in New Zealand* (Wellington, 1940) is still the basic book in its subject, and K. J. Scott, *The New Zealand Constitution* (Oxford, 1962) will undoubtedly remain the major book on constitutional development. As a special contribution to administrative development in modern technological democracies, New Zealand's industrial laws repay study. N. S. Woods has written a comprehensive history of their most significant aspect in his *Industrial Conciliation and Arbitration in New Zealand* (Wellington, 1963).

More detailed reading lists may be found in the appendices to the short histories by Sinclair and by Oliver mentioned above. A select bibliography of New Zealand publications appears annually in the *New Zealand Official Yearbook*. Detailed bibliographies are still needed to supplement the list on pp. 259-90 of *The Cambridge History of the British Empire*, vol. VII, part II (Cambridge, 1933). John Harris's *Guide to New Zealand Reference Material* (2nd ed.; Wellington, 1950) and the supplements by A. G. Bagnall, in the meantime, remain the most comprehensive guide to historical material.

INDEX

Africa, 2, 7, 8, 9, 89
Ahimanawa mountain range, 73
Airy, W. T. G., historian, 22
America, North and South, 23, 31, 34,
    42, 58, 70, 71, 112, 125
Antarctica, 15, 31, 34, 36, 37
Anthony, F. S., author, 77
Apia (Samoa), 34
Ardmore (South Auckland), 30
Argentina, 13, 125
Asia and Southeast Asia, 1. 7, 8, 9, 10,
    11, 13, 15, 31, 34, 37, 83, 105, 125
Auckland, city and province, 1, 21, 23,
    29, 30, 36, 50, 55, 56, 60, 65, 69, 75,
    78, 79, 80, 81, 82, 83, 84, 85, 90,
    91, 92, 94, 136, 142, 145, 146, 160
Australia, 2, 4, 5, 6, 7, 8, 10, 11, 13,
    15, 17, 18, 24, 28, 31, 34, 35, 40, 42,
    58, 59, 60, 61, 63, 70, 72, 79, 80,
    108, 109, 111, 114, 115, 117, 125,
    129, 130, 134, 135, 137, 141, 151,
    158, 161, 162, 171
Ausubel, D., educationist, 45, 46, 89
Avarua (Raratonga), 34
Avon river, 111

Babcock, inventor, 116
Bangkok, 13
Banks Peninsula, 72
Barker, Lady M. A., 76

Bay of Plenty region, 84, 118, 138, 141,
    142, 145
Beaglehole, E., psychologist, 84
Beaglehole, J. C., historian, 25, 27
Beaglehole, Mrs. P., psychologist, 84
Belgium, 13, 108
Bennett, J., anthologist, 52
Blenheim township, 71
Bluff township, 64
Bohemia, 67
Braithwaite, E. R., novelist, 88, 89
Brasch, C., poet, 46
Britain, see Great Britain
British Guiana, 88
Brown, pioneer businessman, 79
Bryce, J., Viscount Bryce, 42
Buck, Sir (Te Rangi Hiroa), anthro-
    pologist, 21, 104
Burma, 11, 13, 31
Butcher, Dr. A. G., educationist, 27
Butler, S., author, 39, 40, 49, 76
Butterworth (Malaysia), 8

California, 24
Campbell, Dr. L., pioneer businessman,
    79
Campbell, W. J., sociologist, 85
Campbell Island, 33
Canada, 5, 6, 7, 8, 10, 12, 13, 28, 34,
    42, 108, 146 163

The Modern Nations in Historical Perspective Series

DATE DUE

APR 20 '70				
FEB 8 '75				
SE 27 '84				
OC 10 '84				

PRINTED IN U.S.A.

GAYLORD